Have you got the Bottle?

A basic guide to Bottle Collectin

By John Woodhams

LONDON LEAGUE PUBLICATIONS LIMITED

Have you got the Bottle?
A basic guide to Bottle Collecting & Digging

Typesetting and layout by Peter Lush.

A CIP catalogue record for this book is available from the British Library.

First published in Great Britain in September 1998 by:
London League Publications Ltd, P.O. Box 10441, London E14 0SB

ISBN: 0-9526064-8-8

Cover design by: Stephen McCarthy Graphic Design
                          23, Carol Street, London NW1 0HT

Printed and bound by: Redwood Books, Trowbridge, Wiltshire.

Cover photos: Front cover John Woodhams
                          Back cover: Bottle Dig: John Woodhams, Bottle display: Peter Lush

Photos: All photos courtesy John Woodhams, except for those by Peter Lush
                          (indicated by PL by the caption)

This book is dedicated to my wife, Margaret, without whom life would not have been so much fun.

Introduction

I am often asked "why would anybody throw away such a lovely ....(whatever it is that has caught the eye)." In fact no matter how attractive an item may be, it is probably only the packaging used by our great grandparents which, like our yoghurt cartons today, was destined to be thrown away when empty.

Bottle collecting took off in England during the late 1960s, when it was realised that a collection of antique bottles and stoneware could be acquired completely free of charge simply by digging them from Victorian and Edwardian rubbish dumps. Soon many thousands of otherwise ordinary people were bitten by the bug and spent their free time excavating these sites and cleaning and displaying their finds.

This peculiar hobby is not just confined to Britain. It is also carried out in New Zealand, Australia, South Africa and America. Surprisingly there is very little bottle digging in Europe, despite their history of packaging being broadly parallel to that of Britain. I have seen French and German Codd bottles and potlids. Huge numbers of French perfumes, colognes and baby feeders were exported and the Dutch produced much of Europe's gin. There are many millions of pounds worth of old bottles still lying buried, waiting for somebody to put in the time and effort to dig them up again.

A national bottle collecting club was formed in the 1970s which was later broken down into smaller regional clubs, some of which are still going. Some closed due to lack of support whilst others have started where demand has warranted it, today there are around 30 clubs dotted around the country from Devon to Scotland.

A number of clubs organise fairs where enthusiasts can dispose of their spares and buy items for their collections. There are now over a dozen established annual shows which range from small affairs with about 20 tables to the Winternational, held every January, which has over 200 stalls. There is even a bi-annual two day national show which attracts visitors from all over the world.

In the 1970s a number of books were available which catered for newcomers to the hobby, the best of these being written by Edward Fletcher and published by Blandford Press. Ted Fletcher reflected the feeling of excitement around at the time, but unfortunately his books are out of print and there is insufficient demand to make it profitable to reprint them. Any books which now appear tend to cover specialist collecting lines and the "quality" items, rather than giving basic information.

This publication grew from a series of articles I was asked to write for beginners to the hobby and its purpose is to give some background into bottle history, production methods, and information on the more popular collecting lines. Hopefully it will also answer some of the questions I am most often asked.

"The Old Bottleman"

In 1978 I was fishing on the River Mole in Surrey and came across some people digging holes in an adjacent field. When I asked one of them what he was doing, he explained that 100 years before the field had been used as a local rubbish dump and that he was digging for old bottles and other artefacts.

I found the idea of digging up antiques intriguing and, fishing forgotten, spent the rest of the day watching the pile of finds increase. The diggers were only too happy to explain what the various bottles were used for and even gave me a couple of common items to take home.

On my next fishing trip I took an extra item, a garden fork, and soon dug my first bottle. From that magic moment it was me that was hooked, not the fish. Regulars on the site introduced me to the Surrey Bottle Collectors Club and since then most of my free time has been spent in digging, cleaning or researching bottles.

For several years I have written an irregular series of articles for club newsletters entitled *"A diggers diary"* as well as the odd article published in magazines such as *"Brewery and Brewerania"* and *"Collecting Doulton"*.

As I dug far more items than I could possibly collect I started selling off my spares at car boot sales where I often heard people say "the old bottle man is here again" - the title has stuck and I became known as "The Old Bottleman" (today the "Old" probably refers to me rather than the bottles).

I am often asked where I go to dig up my bottles. Unfortunately old dumps are becoming harder to find and it is necessary to keep the location of sites secret to prevent them being dug out. I have been on a number of dumps where somebody has told another digger who has passed it on to somebody else, they in turn have told their friends who, in turn has told ...... and so on. The two best sites I ever dug were both stripped in a matter of weeks because somebody could not keep a secret. However, all over the country there are still thousands of old rubbish dumps to be found by anybody prepared to look for them. (If anybody needs help to dig a site I **can** keep a secret)

I am extremely fortunate in having an understanding wife who also collects (blue and white dolls china). She often accompanies me on my digging trips, but is convinced that I am just a grown up little boy whose bottle digging is just an excuse to get dirty.

However deeply you go into the collecting hobby, whether you buy bottles or dig them yourself, the most important aspects are to have fun collecting and to enjoy your collection.

John Woodhams
September 1998

Thank you

We would like to thank Margaret for her support and hospitality, Dave Farrar for his help in checking information and support during the production process, Sandra for help in proof reading, Stuart Alexander of Redwood Books, the advertisers for their support and everyone who ordered the book in advance.

Prices

This book is not intended to be a price guide and I have omitted to give any values except in broad terms, or for top of the range items.

In the world of bottle collecting prices are not fixed but can rise or fall almost overnight and a value given today may well be out of date in a month or two. Diggers on a large dump often bring enough finds onto the market to cause values to fall, whilst the opposite will happen when the site is finished.

With the availability of bottles fluctuating between feast and famine, a fixed price guide is obviously out of the question. With such a volatile market, the only possible form in which a price guide could last for a time is where items are put into price bands (£1-5, £5-10 etc.) and show comparative rather than fixed values. Whenever this type of format has been used in the past, there has always been controversy over whether items are correctly banded, and availability (or lack of) can move items into different bands quite quickly. At any bottle collecting fair the same items can be found on a number of stalls, each being priced differently.

The two factors which determine a value are rarity and condition. Surprisingly, age has little bearing on this. Some hundred year old mineral water bottles change hands for over £1,000, yet it is still possible to buy a 300 year old wine bottle for a tenth of that price. Locality can play a large part in determining value, a mundane ginger beer bottle sold for £10 in one part of the country can fetch ten times that elsewhere if it is a scarce local item. Dutch auctions are quite common, with unusual items being touted from collector to collector in an attempt to jack up the final selling price.

During the past few years there has been growing interest in buying and selling better quality pieces through specialist bottle auctions. These seem to attract unusually high prices for rarities and estimates of many items are wildly inaccurate. I can see this trend continuing as results of sales and prices realised are starting to be reported in antique trade publications which can only help boost the popularity of these sales.

I am a firm believer in the maxim that it is the buyer who sets the price, an item is only worth what somebody is prepared to pay for it, and not a penny more, no matter what value the seller may put on it. Many dealers seem to think that a bottle is worth whatever price they decide to put on it. They are the ones who bring the same items to show after show, their stock is so overpriced that it will never sell.

Every collecting line seems to have its own band of specialists who are willing to pay almost anything to get hold of ultra rare items and anybody now wishing to collect the "top of the range" items will need very deep pockets.

Here are a few examples of prices that have been paid: mineral water £1,000+, ginger beer £900+, potlid £3,000+, cream pot £1,900, poison £6,700, ink bottle £2,000, and a milk bottle has fetched £162. However these prices are exceptional and must be seen as such. It would take quite a large warehouse to display examples of all the different bottles and pots in the 25p to £5 price range. Personally I only keep items that appeal to me and I am not in the least bothered that some of my treasures are only worth a couple of pounds.

The author (before the beard) at home with a few of the items in his collection

Contents

Tel: 0181-898-9507
24hrs Answerphone

JOHN WOODHAMS
THE OLD BOTTLEMAN

VICTORIAN AND EDWARDIAN
BOTTLES & STONEWARE SPECIALIST

SATURDAY & SUNDAY 9AM - 5:30PM
THE STABLES ANTIQUE CENTRE
THE STABLES MARKET
CHALK FARM ROAD
CAMDEN LOCK.
NEAREST TUBE STATION CHALK FARM.

Regularly changing stock covering a wide range of items including:-

GLASS: *Beers, Baby Feeders, Blue & green Poisons, Inks, Medicines & Cures, Mineral Waters, Perfumes, Sauces & Whiskies.*

STONEWARE: *Blacking Pots, Creams, Flagons, Ginger Jars, Inks, Marmalades, Polishes & Storage Jars.*

PRINTED STONEWARE: *Caviars, Cream pots, Ginger Beers, Fish & Meat Pastes, Food Jars, Mustards & Ointments.*

POTLIDS: *Meat & Fish Pastes, Cold Creams, Toothpastes.*

Large Quantities of stock held. Enquire about shipping orders or pub and restaurant decorations.

Part I

Building a Collection

Chapter 1: A Brief History of Glass

The true history of glass-making is lost in the mists of time. However, it is generally accepted that it goes back well over two thousand years to the time of the ancient Egyptians. They used techniques of coiling and core moulding to produce small quantities of crude, but serviceable, containers.

The story was taken several stages further by the Romans who produced medicine phials, perfume bottles, vases and decanters. These were core moulded, free-blown and even made in clay moulds. The skills they developed spread with their empire and remains of Roman glassworks have been found over much of Europe.

Glass-making almost died out in Britain during the 1300 years following the Roman occupation, although there were a few cottage industries making small amounts of decorative items. The art was mainly kept alive by a number of monasteries whose output was mostly window glass, but their knowledge was all but lost during the first half of the 16th century when Henry VIII abolished the monastic orders.

Some 50 years later commercial glass-making was re-introduced by European immigrants who established their small industries in the south of England. There they found both abundant raw materials and the forests necessary to provide fuel for the furnaces. The furnaces were usually build on the side of a slope so that any wind would cause an up-draught to assist combustion.

The ingredients used for glass at that time were very basic, just sand mixed with lime and potash, the potash being obtained from the burnt wood used to fuel the furnaces. The mixture was put in a metal container (crucible) and melted in the furnace, it was then allowed to cool to the consistency of treacle when it could be shaped. Since the raw materials were unrefined they contained many impurities. The most common was iron which oxidised in the process and gave the finished product a distinctive green colour which, depending on the amount present, could range from a slight tinge to being deep enough to make the glass appear black.

Glass-making was a very small scale affair for the next 200 years or so, being generally concentrated in the southern counties of England. The main products were window glass and decorative items for the wealthier homes, together with small numbers of medicine phials and apothecary jars. Bristol developed into the country's main area for glass production, in 1696 it had nine glassworks of which six were involved in bottle making (by this time wine bottles were being manufactured). The area grew in importance and by the latter part of the 1700s thousands of bottles were being produced to hold St. Vincent waters (also known as Bristol waters) which were sold as a cure for diabetes and other complaints.

The cobalt blue glass often used for producing poison bottles is frequently referred to as "Bristol Blue" by antique dealers due to this association between early bottle making and Bristol.

A boom in glass-making came about with the industrial revolution. Until then the lives of most workers centred on small towns and villages, most of their food being supplied by local farms. The general movement of the population from the countryside to the manufacturing centres resulted in a need to improve the distribution of food as the influx of people outstripped local production. Traditional methods of preserving food were turned into small industries enabling it to be brought in from further afield. At this time grocery stores had most of their supplies delivered in bulk and measured or weighed it out to the customers' needs. As the century progressed there was a gradual change to packaging in portions such as a pound of jam or a pint of vinegar, much of the produce being supplied in glass or stoneware jars and bottles.

With the growth of a fast and efficient railway network it became possible to transport food from all over the country, with delivery being fast enough to ensure that the food did not spoil in transit. In the 1890s one Devonshire dairy (Harris) had a small picture of a train on their cream pots with the legend "per rail daily".

Soft drinks and ginger beers

The mid 1800s saw a huge new growth industry in bottled soft drinks and ginger beers. The biggest single cost in drink production was the price of the container and suppliers would re-use them as often as possible (rather like our milk bottles today). A number of suppliers tried to get their customers to return bottles by charging a deposit, usually a farthing (1/4 penny) which was refunded when the bottle was returned. Initially there was a lot of resentment against paying this charge and some firms advertised that the bottle was free, sometimes it carried the words "No deposit charged". The age of packaging and the throwaway society had arrived.

By the 1870s the two piece bottle making mould was in general use, simplifying manufacturing and enabling mass production to take place. Hundreds of thousands of bottles were being made annually for preserved fruits and jams, pickles, sauces, mineral waters, beers, wines and spirits, poisons, inks, medicines, etc. The quantity steadily increased until the peak was reached in the early 1940s by which time all bottles were being produced by automatic bottle making machines.

Some idea of the numbers of bottles produced can be gained from records showing that in 1866 there were 6,000 tons and 2.5 million bottle corks imported (mainly from Portugal) - and this was only the start of the boom in bottle making.

Although the machine was invented in the early part of the twentieth century, it did not come into general use until the 1920s and took about ten years to fully replace hand blown production methods.

The next generation of machines were able to produce bottles with an external screw thread to take a metal (or Bakelite) cap. It also brought about a huge improvement in quality control ensuring that each item was exactly the same as the previous one and the one before that. Although some containers were still embossed with product details and the supplier's name, the many flaws and colour variations associated with traditional production methods were eradicated and bottles lost their individuality.

The introduction of the automatic bottle making machine is seen by most collectors as being the dividing line which decides what is, and what is not, collectable - few machine made bottles are worth keeping, with only a tiny number being worth more than a pound or so. Bottle diggers working 1930s dumps generally leave the bulk of their glassware behind at the end of the day. The main exceptions being the blue and green poisons which occasionally turn up and the wide mouthed milk bottles whose prices are being slowly pushed up by an increasing demand. (However, these sites are still worth digging as figurines, cake decorations, advertising pieces and footwarmers are often found in greater numbers than on earlier dumps).

Bottle making methods

Coiled

A simple technique in which a rope of semi-molten glass was wrapped around a clay core. Once the basic shape had been formed it was reheated and smoothed by rolling it on a stone slab. The item was then allowed to cool and the clay core chipped out.

Core Moulded

A clay model of the item was dipped into molten glass and allowed to cool. It was the dipped again and the process repeated until there was sufficient thickness of glass to allow the clay mould to be chipped away. Both this and coiling resulted in thick walled articles which were more suitable for decorative purposes.

Free Blown

Before the arrival of the mould, a bottle's shape depended on the craftsman's skill. The method involved the glassblower taking a blob of molten glass on to one end of an iron tube or blowing iron and inflating it by blowing down the tube (rather like blowing up a balloon). Further shaping was carried out by turning or spinning the blowing iron and by rolling the glass on a metal sheet. Sometimes callipers were used to measure the diameter of glass in finer pieces such as drinking vessels and their use can sometimes be seen in the form fine grooves around the walls of the glass. Most bottles were measured by eye which gave variations in shape to the individual items in a batch.

Once the body and neck had been formed, a solid metal rod (pontil rod) was stuck to the bottom of the bottle with a small blob of molten glass and the blowing iron broken away. Using the pontil rod to hold the bottle, the top of the neck was put into the furnace, heated and the lip shaped. Early wine bottles had loose fitting corks so were given a collar (string rim) just below the lip which was used to secure the twine which held the cork in place. Later wine bottles were sealed with a tight fitting cork and needed a thick collar of glass to withstand the pressure of having the cork hammered into place.

When the bottle was completed the pontil rod was broken away leaving a lump of rough glass on the base. This sharp end was liable to scratch the surface of a polished table and early wines were sometimes supplied in a wickerwork cradle or osier. The problem was overcome by giving wine bottles a concave base, or kick-up. The pontil mark was often ground away on small bottles such as perfumes which had flat bases. Today it is still possible to see these skills in action in the small glassworks dotted around the country, many have viewing galleries and are well advertised at holiday centres as tourist attractions. The methods and tools they use are the same as those employed over a period of several centuries.

Mould Blown

The first patent covering a mould for bottle-making was taken out by Joseph Ricketts in 1821, due to this he has been credited with inventing the mould. However moulds were in use long before. In 1752 a man was charged (and acquitted) at Newgate with stealing a brass bottle mould valued at 18 shillings from a Mr. Thomas Warren and Company of Temple Street, Bristol. However there are no records relating to early moulds and it is generally accepted by collectors that the Ricketts was the first mould to come into general use.

As can be seen, the mould was directly below the craftsman and opened and closed by two foot pedals. Early bottles were embossed "H. RICKETTS & CO. GLASSWORKS BRISTOL", (note the connection with Bristol, still an important centre for bottle making). The finished item had three seam lines, but it is not unusual to find three piece moulded bottles without these distinctive marks as makers sometimes disguised the seams by turning the glass in the mould as it was blown.

RICKETTS MOULD

MOULD DETAILS

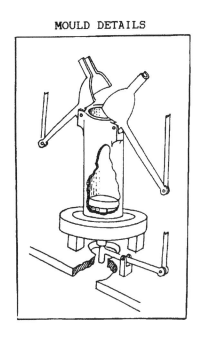

BASAL EMBOSSING

Ricketts' patent was a breakthrough in manufacturing which, for the first time, made it possible to produce a batch of bottles with similar dimensions and capacities, but it was far too cumbersome for making the smaller sized bottles such as medicines, sauces and inks. By the middle of the century small two and three piece hinged moulds had appeared on the scene which revolutionised bottle making and, by the mid 1860s, had largely replaced the Ricketts moulds.

These small moulds made bottle manufacturing much easier and it became possible to mass produce bottles quickly and cheaply, either in a large range of stock sizes or to special order. Standard shaped bottles could be used for a wide range of products (rather like our plastic cartons today, the same shape is used for coleslaw, yoghurt, cream or fromage frais). I have Victorian advertising illustrating similar shaped bottles being used for liniment and straw hat dye.

For a small extra charge bottles could be personalised to meet an individual customer's requirements by embossing details of the supplier or the product on the bottle. Embossing was produced by putting an engraved metal plate into the mould, the lettering being engraved into the plate in reverse.

Most engravers were superb craftsmen, but some were illiterate and treated letters as shapes to be copied. This sometimes led to occasional spelling mistakes and for the odd letter to be engraved the wrong way round.

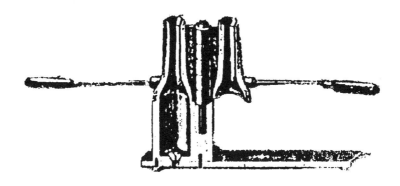

A typical two piece hinged mould

Newcomers are sometimes surprised to see bottles for sale which appear to have their tops broken. These are not damaged, but were actually produced with sharp jagged lips and this is a quite normal finish for many Victorian bottles. In fact almost all bottles until around 1920 had this type of top at some stage in manufacturing.

To make a mould blown bottle the glassblower took a blob of molten glass on the end of the blowing rod and put it in a heated mould which was then closed and the bottle blown into shape. Finally he would blow a small bubble just outside the top of the mould which was allowed to burst and break away the blowing rod. The mould was then opened and the bottle removed, at this stage it had a jagged top or "burst lip".

This sharp lip was often left on bottles which were used for cheaper products such as inks or sauces as the profit margin on the product was not sufficient to justify the cost of improving the top. These bottles were sealed with a cork which the sharp top bit into helping to keep it in place. Ink bottles were sometimes made airtight by having wax poured over their tops and sauce bottle tops might be wrapped with foil.

Another method of removing the blowing iron was to cut through the semi molten glass with a pair of shears which gave a much neater finish. But using shears was a separate operation and the resultant bottles were a little more expensive and the method was not used too often. Although this is a true shear top finish, amongst collectors both these and jagged tops are generally known as shear tops.

A selection of "sheared top" bottles

Bottles which required a tight fitting cork, such as medicines and poison bottles, had their lips re-heated and flattened to give a collar which provided extra strength.

Mineral water and beer bottles had corks hammered into place and needed strengthening to prevent them splitting under the pressure. The tops were heated and a blob of molten glass added, this was shaped either with special tools or by rolling on a wooden block. Sometimes it is possible to see the wood grain transferred into the lip of the bottle, appearing like irregular lines running around the top. Occasionally the glass from added lips runs down the neck of the bottle rather like wax runs down the side of a candle. When held up to the light, it is often possible to see the original burst lip which looks rather like a crack running through the added top. This type of bottle is known as a "Blob Top"

ADDED TOP BOTTLES

The original ·tops look like cracks in the glass

The operation of blowing bottles into moulds seems a simple and straightforward operation, but it required a good working knowledge of glass, a great deal of experience and a strong pair of lungs to blow bottles continuously for up to 16 hours a day. The mundane task of keeping the moulds at the correct temperature was given to a boy. If the mould was too cool it gave the glass a rough finish, but if it was too hot then glass tended to stick to it.

Children from eight years old worked the same hours as craftsmen until 1830 when the age was raised to 12. There was very little formal training, if a youngster wished to learn the trade his skills would be picked up by watching the tradesmen and spending his short meal breaks practising.

Glassworks' employees were usually paid on a piecework basis, earning a set amount per gross (12 dozen) bottles made, and speed was an important factor in manufacture. Most craftsmen were highly skilled but their ability was often wasted by the factory system used to keep costs down and production up. Cheap raw materials, high output, long hours, low wages, poor working conditions and minimal quality control all combined to make an end product which was little better than just good enough to do the job.

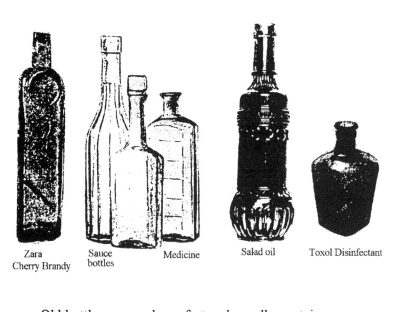

| Zara Cherry Brandy | Sauce bottles | Medicine | Salad oil | Toxol Disinfectant |

ROSE'S
Lime Juice

Old bottles are rarely perfect and usually contain one or more of the following flaws: a rough texture, bits of grit in the walls, be full of air bubbles, contain odd lumps and bumps in their surfaces, have sides of varying thickness, have blobs of glass adhering to their seams (sometimes being razor sharp), the glass may contain odd splashes of colour (often brown), the walls may sag, the neck may be offset, or the whole bottle could be generally misshapen. To those who are accustomed to modern production methods, where the slightest flaw is a reason for rejection, the above might appear to be a list of points to beware of, but it is precisely these flaws which give old bottles charm and nostalgic appeal and make them so collectable.

Personally I find today's glass is too perfect to be interesting and even coloured glass seems to be sterile and lack character. Top quality glass is too uniform to make an interesting display and far to expensive to take the risk of actually using it (but then my wife tells me I am a bit of a Philistine).

Examining seam lines is one way to tell whether a bottle is old, or before about 1920 when bottle making machines first came into use. Machine made bottles have a seam running the full length from base to lip, in mould blown bottles the seam lines die out between the shoulder and the lip. Also the hand blowing of containers from the thick treacle like molten glass gives bottles much thicker walls than those produced in a machine. Air bubbles and other flaws are common in old bottles and this extra thickness was desirable to give additional strength.

Coloured Glass

Victorian glass was coloured by the addition of natural elements and chemicals to the mix. The final depth of colour depends not only on the amount of colouring agent used, but also on the thickness of the glass. As its name implies, the highly collectable cobalt blue glass (known as Bristol blue in the antiques trade) was obtained by the addition of cobalt. Light blue (sometimes called ice blue) was arrived at by using Copper Oxide.

The black glass used to make early wine bottles is in fact a very deep green and was made by the use of iron oxide. Iron was naturally present in the raw materials of that time but it was common practice to further darken the glass, one reason being to prevent purchasers from seeing the sediment in the bottom of the bottle. This colour was also ideal for bottling products, such as truffles, which would spoil if exposed to light.

A lighter green needed borate of lime. Some bottles were made from an opaque white glass called milk glass which was obtained by mixing in tin oxide or zinc oxide. The glass could be also be given a greenish or bluish tinge by adding in copper oxide, the final colour depending on both the amount added and the firing temperature.

The distinctive bottles used to hold Odol (mouthwash) were made in milkglass. Odol registered the shape of the bottle with the Patent office to try to stop competitors using a similar bottle and cashing in on the product's popularity. "Patent" or "Flask Patented" is sometimes embossed on these bottles' base.

The most expensive colour to produce was red, a light red could be made by adding copper oxide and firing at high temperature, but this required a large amount of costly fuel. Deep ruby red was even more expensive to produce since it needed a small amount of gold in the mix. The high cost ensured that red colours were reserved for decorative items and perfume flasks rather than bottles.

Few Victorian bottles were produced in clear glass as this was another costly business requiring the addition of manganese imported from South Africa. There was also another drawback, it often turned a pale purple or pink when exposed to ultra violet light for long periods. The sun's rays in Europe were usually not strong enough to cause any problems, but special care had to be taken with storage of bottles exported to parts of America, Australia and South Africa. It became impossible to import manganese during the 1914-1918 War and other alternatives such as selenium and arsenic were used, some of today's clear glass still uses selenium.

Chapter 2: Household Bottles

Household bottles are not a recognised collecting line. The title has been used to group together some of the huge range of bottle types which loosely fall into this category.

A century ago many staple products came in rather plain pots, jars or bottles. Since these were sold in huge quantities, they turn up in relatively large numbers and change hands for fairly modest prices. Due to their ready availability and fairly plain design there are few collectors specialising in these day to day items, but just because they are common it should not detract from their important place in packaging history.

I feel that there is too much store set on rarity and believe that it is not necessary for an item to be one of only a handful known to make it attractive. The easy availability of the well known bottle embossed with the simple legend "Lung Tonic" does not make it any less interesting than if it were a scarce local medicine.

Samples

These are usually miniature copies of full size bottles, sometimes being embossed "Sample" or "Free Sample". Today's samples rarely come free. It is usually either necessary to purchase another product from a company to get the "free" sample attached to the packaging, or to buy the item then post off a till receipt to get a refund. However, 50 or 100 years ago samples could be obtained free by sending stamps for the postage.

Most samples seem to come in aqua or clear glass, but they are a good line to collect for a small space. The bottles are too small to have held anything other than a minute paper label and instead are often embossed on several sides. I have a small rectangular bottle in green glass embossed "Free sample Izal disinfectant" one word on each panel. Many samples once held sauces or coffees but I have others for products as diverse as Mason's wine essence, Virol (a preparation of bone marrow for invalids), Mellins Infant food, Roses lime cordial and a split soda Hamilton (see mineral waters).

A good way of filling out a collection of samples is to add some of the more unusual shaped miniature spirits bottles sold at the larger off-licences.

Rose's Lime Juice   H.P. Sauce   Liquer bottle   Coffee sample   Idris Cordial

Sauces and Coffees

This is a line where a collection can be gathered for very little cost, few of these bottles will have a price higher than £5.00. Most coffees and sauces are tall bottles with long necks and square section bodies.

Most coffee was sold in a liquid form, usually with chicory being added, helping fill out the bottle and to impart a sharp taste. The bottles were usually much the same shape as sauces but with added tops, they were sealed with glass stoppers with a cork ring fitted to make them airtight.

The two sizes of Camp Coffee are the most common bottles found, others which often turn up are Lyons, Symingtons and two sizes of CWS in a dark green glass. There are some nice fluted sauces to be found and others with ornate necks, (some of these actually contained vinegar).

Sauces were very popular, one reason was that they helped disguise the taste of tainted meat. Early bottles were shear topped, later they were given added tops. The most commonly found examples are:- Daddies Favourite (later Daddies), Indian, Worcestershire, Gartons HP (today called HP sauce), Grill, Yorkshire Relish and Fletchers Tomato Sauce.

Meat Extracts

There is a huge range to be collected and most makers used several different sized bottles for their products. The best known are the brown glass Bovril jars in various shades which appear in 16, eight, four, two, one and half ounce sizes. Bottles had long necks and were sealed with a flat cork. Around 1930 the necks became shorter and in the late 1930s lugs were

moulded onto the lip to take a metal cap. Black glass bottles with a hole in the base were used for advertising and between 1910 and 1915 a green glass bottle appeared. It is possible to find over 20 different bottles from just one company.

Due to Bovril's popularity, other companies also used brown glass for their bottles and frequently made them similar in shape. Oxo in a range of sizes and the later Marmite jars are good examples.

My favourite extract bottle is the individual shaped Valentine's Meat Juice. There is a belief that this was the bottle which started collecting in Britain. The story goes that somebody found one by the side of the Grand Union Canal at Iver (Buckinghamshire) and was so intrigued that he searched around, found a number of different bottles and eventually started to dig for them. The tale is probably untrue but the bottle has found its niche in bottle collecting history.

Today we use Bovril (and Marmite) as flavouring for stews and to spread on buttered bread. Originally meat extracts were advertised as making a healthy drink which was ideally suitable for invalids. A few companies combined the product with wine as an alcoholic medicinal tonic which was sold in large bottles.

Hair Restorers and Colourings

Like today, many men (and some ladies) worried about losing their hair. This led to individuals claiming that they were able to cure baldness and the use of clever advertising enabled them to sell their magical preparations to a gullible public. Others wanted their hair coloured to disguise greyness and a range of hair colorants was also produced and sold

Hair restorers can make a colourful collection, few were supplied in aqua glass, most being sold in coloured bottles which helped to catch the eye of prospective customers. They can be found in amber, brown, blue and green glass.

Some have exotic names such as the bottle shown on the right - The Mexican Hair Renewer (for bald Mexicans?), Koko for the hair, Madam Girade's hygienic hair restorer and Lockyer's Sulphur hair restorer which must have smelled awful and looked rather peculiar when applied to a bald head.

GROW BEAUTIFUL HAIR FREE!

A SUGGESTION ALL MAY ADOPT.

Distribution of 1,000,000 Four-Fold Hair-Health and Beauty Outfits FREE.

HERE is a great opportunity and a valuable gift for every reader of this paper.

If you desire to look young and well-groomed, look to your hair. That is why the proprietors of the world-famous Hair-Growing Specific "Harlene" are offering 1,000,000 Outfits Free.

Here is a suggestion for you to adopt. Send for your "Harlene Hair-Drill" Four-Fold Gift and grow healthy, luxuriant, and abundant hair. Why not decide to-day to banish hair poverty for ever? Why wear attenuated, thin, impoverished, lifeless locks of hair when all the rich sparkle and abundance of hair in its natural healthy condition is you · for the asking?

ACCEPT THIS WONDERFUL GIFT.

There is no restriction to this gift distribution. It is sufficient that you are troubled with any form of hair "ailment," or that you desire to improve the appearance of your hair.

The Gift parcel comprises :

1. A bottle of "Harlene," the true liquid food for the hair, which stimulates it to new growth. It is Tonic, Food, and Dressing in one.

2. A packet of the marvellous hair and scalp-cleansing "Cremex" Shampoo Powder, which prepares the head for "Hair Drill."

3. A bottle of "Uzon" Brilliantine, which gives a final touch of beauty to the hair, and is especially beneficial to those whose scalp is "dry."

4. A copy of the new edition of the "Hair-Drill" Manual, giving complete Instructions.

No hair trouble can defy the soothing, strengthening 'effect of "Harlene" and its scientific method of application, "Hair-drill."

MILLIONS PRACTISE HAIR-DRILL.

Millions of men and women now practise

"Harlene Hair-Drill" daily. They have tested and proved that this unique preparation, "Harlene," and its agreeable method of application, "Hair-Drill," is the surest way to overcome all hair defects, and that it is also the easiest way to ensure the perfect growth of long, silky, beautiful hair in abundance, glossy and bright.

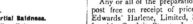

It is wonderful what a difference only 2 minutes a day practice of "Harlene Hair-Drill" will achieve in the cultivation and preservation of a glorious head of hair. Friends and relations long absent will wonder at the beneficial change. Try it free for one week. Accept one of the 1,000,000 Free Four-fold Gift Outfits offered to readers to-day. Simply send Coupon below with your name and address and 4d. stamps for return postage and packing of parcel.

There is therefore no need to continue to suffer from

1. **Scalp Irritation.**
2. **Complete or Partial Baldness.**
3. **Thinning or Falling Hair.**
4. **Splitting Hairs.**
5. **Over Greasiness.**
6. **Scurf or Dandruff.**
7. **Unruly, Wiry Hair.**

Young women can maintain their hair in abundant beauty, and men and women of more mature years can regain all the lost lustre and health, whether it arises from illness, worry, overwork, or the passing of years.

THE "HARLENE" WAY

First of all cleanse the hair and scalp

with a delightful "Cremex" Shampoo—there is no more pleasant, invigorating toilet exercise. Then sprinkle the hair with "Harlene," and gently massage the roots of the hair with your finger-tips. Then add a few drops of "Uzon" Brilliantine to give the hair a final touch of brilliance.

Prove the wonderful merits of "Harlene" for yourself without cost. The gifts referred to above will be sent you immediately you post the coupon below.

HARLENE FOR MEN

ALSO

Every man desires to preserve a fresh, smart, crisp appearance, and in this respect the care of the hair is essential. The Free Gift Offer made in this announcement is open to every man, and they will find this two-minutes-a-day "Harlene Hair-Drill" a delightfully pleasant and beneficial toilet exercise.

After a Free Trial you will be able to obtain supplies of "Harlene" from your chemist at 1s. 1½d., 2s. 9d., or 4s. 9d. per bottle.

"Uzon" Brilliantine costs 1s. and 2s. 6d. per bottle, and "Cremex" Shampoo Powders 1s. 1½d. per box of seven shampoos (single each).

Any or all of the preparations will be sent post free on receipt of price direct from Edwards' Harlene, Limited, 20, 22, 24, 26 Lamb's Conduit Street, London, W.C.1. Carriage extra on foreign orders. Cheques and P.O.'s should be crossed.

HARLENE GIFT COUPON

FREE Detach and Post to EDWARDS' HARLENE, Ltd., 20, 22, 24 and 26 Lamb's Conduit Street, London, W.C.1.

Dear Sirs,—Please send me your Free "Harlene" Four-Fold Hair Growing Outfit as announced. I enclose 4d. in stamps for postage and packing.

NOTE TO READER.

Write your full name and address clearly on a plain piece of paper, pin this Coupon to it, and post as directed above. (Mark envelope "Sample Dept.")

Canada in Khaki, Dec., 1917.

This advertisement is from 1916. The smaller bottle is embossed with the words "Harlene for the hair" on the front and the word "Sample" on the sides. Both sizes of bottle are quite often found in rubbish dumps up to the mid 1920s.

Cordial Bottles

Some of the lime cordial bottles are heavily embossed with lime plants growing up around the bottle. The best example is the one used by L. Rose and Co at the turn of the century (today Roses lime cordial is still a popular brand). Although normally seen in the large size, around 14 inches high, a range of smaller sizes turn up right down to about five inches. Miniature black glass examples are known but these are extremely rare and can fetch over £75. A large size in black glass version is also found in Australia.

Other companies using embossed climbing limes include Stowers who used a capital S and a tower as a trademark and Schweppes, who also use a fountain as a trademark on some of their bottles

There are a number of cordial bottles around which are moulded in unusual shapes, such as one that looks like a huge thistle, others are embossed so heavily that they have the appearance of frosted glass

There were several companies supplying their drinks in the form of fruit flavoured sugar crystals, most of these turning up in similar shaped square section bottles about four inches tall

The best known type is the Eiffel Tower brand by Foster Clarke & Co. of Maidstone who produced lemonade and fruit drinks. The earliest bottles from the company carry a picture of the Eiffel Tower and are quite scarce. Other common bottles are those from Carter's Big Wheel brand of Bristol, Bird's and Syston's of Cambridge and Simons's from London S.E.

Mason's of Nottingham used attractive mid blue bottles for their wine essences which came in a variety of flavours. The cost was six pence, a bottle supposedly made 60 glasses. Mason's essence was also used as flavouring in cooking.

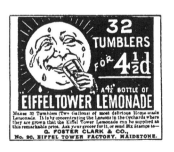

Veterinary Bottles

This group has a small following, usually being collected by those in the trade and being used to decorate surgeries. The most prolific supplier was Day and Sons, Later becoming Day Son and Hewitt. The company made a wide range of products and used several different coloured glass bottles. One of my friends has a collection which includes wooden boxes used to supply the medicines to vets.

One unusual shape which often turns up is a six sided aqua bottle which is embossed on two panels Benbow's Dog Mixture. I cannot find out what this was meant to cure, the product was very popular but appears not to have been advertised.

The most common veterinary bottle found is a round, glass stoppered bottle which is usually heavily embossed with the wording "Ellirmans' embrocation for horses, Manufactory, Slough". The company also made an embrocation for humans and they advertised both this and the variety for horses at the same time.

Adverts for different household products from the 1880s

Chapter 3: Glass

Wine Bottles

Two of most popular wines drunk in Britain in the latter half of the 1500s were Spanish sack and French claret, both of which were supplied in barrels. At that time glass bottles were available, made in France and imported empty to be filled by vintners when the wine was sold. The first English glassworks producing wine bottles was in London in 1592. But this embryonic industry had a difficult time getting established due to French competition.

King James the First gave some protection by banning the import of French wine bottles in 1592. However, this was to prove short-lived as potteries soon complained about the amount of business being lost to glassworks. Other industries were also complaining about the huge number of trees being burnt for fuel to feed the furnaces and in 1636 the sale of wine in glass bottles was completely banned.

Obviously this ban was a severe blow to manufacturers, but it was to prove an important step for bottle collectors today. The ban only covered the sale of wine supplied in bottles. It was perfectly legal to buy wine by the barrel and have it decanted into one's own bottles by the wine merchant. This loophole was exploited by the rich who could afford to have bottles made for them. In places, it became something of a status symbol to provide guests with wine poured from a glass bottle.

Sealed Bottles

When a customer had his own bottles made he could ask for them to be marked to indicate ownership. This was carried out by putting a blob of glass on the shoulder or body of the bottle and, whilst still semi molten, impressing a design or lettering into it with a metal stamp. The resulting flat circular disc is called a seal and a bottle carrying this is known as a sealed bottle.

Markings on a seal could take a number of forms but were usually one or more of the following: a name or initials, a coat of arms, a heraldic device or a date. This date is not necessarily the year a bottle was made but could denote a special anniversary for which the bottle had been made, or even the vintage of the wine it contained.

Typical seals

18th century
sealed wine

Some tavern owners used a picture representing the name of their establishment. One example of this is a bottle whose seal carries a picture of a mermaid, the date 1682 and the letter "A H". This has been identified as belonging to Anthony Hall, the proprietor of the Mermaid tavern (in Oxford) in 1682.

The oldest recorded seal is dated 1632 and carries the name John Jefferson, unfortunately only the seal itself exists. The earliest complete bottle is in the Northampton County Museum, dated 1657, it bears the initials RPM and a profile of a head wearing a crown.

The addition of a seal can increase a bottle's value 20-fold and most are now sold through the bigger auction houses, rather than by private sales between collectors. Between 1650 and 1850 the wine bottle gradually changed its shape and it is possible to give a fairly accurate dating to an early bottle simply from its shape.

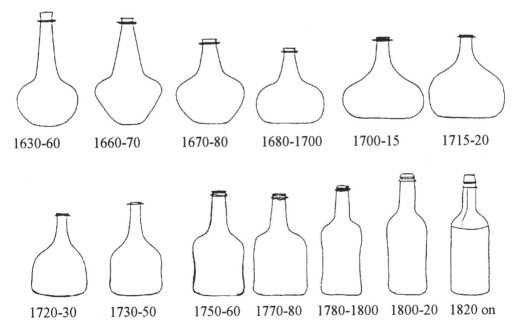

| 1630-60 | 1660-70 | 1670-80 | 1680-1700 | 1700-15 | 1715-20 |

| 1720-30 | 1730-50 | 1750-60 | 1770-80 | 1780-1800 | 1800-20 | 1820 on |

Ink Bottles

The first thing to say about ink bottles is that many so called inks actually contained some other product. It is probable that many, if not all, bell shapes actually contained gum for gluing paper and it is known that a "Birdcage" ink held perfume. However, small details like this tend to be ignored by collectors of this particular line. It is generally accepted that the category of inks includes not only those bottles which actually contained ink, but also some that look as if they should have held it.

Until the middle of the nineteenth century ink was commonly sold in a powdered form and mixed with water when required for use. The steel nibbed pen was available early in the century but at that time quills were still in general use. It was not until the 1840s, when Joseph Gilliot promoted its use, that the steel nibbed pen started to become accepted as THE writing instrument. Manufacturers of pens received an unexpected boost with the introduction of the universal penny post which helped bring letter writing into fashion.

By the 1850s ink was starting to be supplied ready mixed in liquid form, saving the inconvenient and messy business of mixing ink powder. Soon there were scores of manufacturers competing for a share of an expanding market, some of them selling their products in odd shaped bottles in an attempt to attract the customer's attention.

Glass Ink Bottles

Fierce competition forced bottle manufacturers to keep overheads to a minimum in order to survive, one saving was to supply bottles in a range of standard shapes. This applied to ink bottles as well as other products such as mineral waters and medicines. The most common shaped ink was squat with six sides, although both the rectangular (boat) and square shapes were almost as popular. These both had grooves formed on either side of the neck to serve as pen rests.

Six Sided   Square   Rectangular (Boat)

Most ink bottles were sheared lipped and sealed with a cork, some suppliers poured wax over the cork to provide an airtight seal and prevent evaporation of the contents. The standard price for a bottle of ink was one old penny, when the cost of the bottle, its contents, a cork, label, transport and the shopkeeper's profit had all been taken out, there was little left for the manufacturer. Few could afford the additional cost of having the suppliers name embossed on the bottle and inks are generally plain.

A small number of companies regularly used embossed bottles. The best known are Field's (inks and gums) in a range of sizes, Stephens Inks, Lyons, Morrell (in various designs), Moncrieff, Blackwood, J.R. and Pridge. There is an especially nice example from Swan Ink with a trademark of a swan and I have seen a square bottle embossed with the legend " Free Sample" which, surprisingly, fails to show a supplier's name.

| Tent | Barrel | Birdcage | Derby All British (Waxed cork) |

At the upper end of the market packaging played an important part in determining sales. Manufacturers tended to use a better quality of bottle for their product, often using coloured glass for the different coloured inks. Following aqua, the most common colours are green, blue and amber, with shades ranging from the merest hint of colour to being so deep as to appear almost black. The novelty of using a bottle made in an unusual shape could also help sales. Some are superb examples of the bottle makers (or the mould makers) skills, only in miniature. It was possible to buy ink in small globes with a map of the world on the surface or a little cottage complete with windows, a tiled roof and a water barrel.

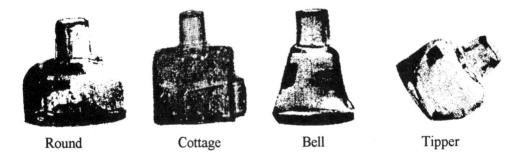

| Round | Cottage | Bell | Tipper |

The tipper ink shown above was designed for use with fountain pens. When some of the ink had been used the bottle was tipped on its side so that the pen could be filled without any air getting into it.

Nowadays some inks can fetch ludicrously high prices, sometimes in excess of £300, it is rumoured that a cobalt blue cottage ink sold for £2,000. As in all collecting lines these prices are exceptional and it is still possible to build up a large collection for quite a modest outlay - one collector is reputed to have 2,000 different ink bottles and is apparently still adding more.

Stoneware Ink Bottles

The use of stoneware bottles was generally reserved for the sale of larger quantities (or bulk) ink. To save on money, schools and offices bought their ink in large bottles and poured it into the individual inkwells. Most of these larger containers are stoneware with either a white or a saltglazed finish, glass examples turn up occasionally but these are less common. Bulk inks come in a wide range of sizes ranging between four and ten inches in height. Other sizes are sometimes found but these are more unusual, I have one in my collection which is less than two inches tall and only held a couple of tablespoons of ink.

Most bottles had a pouring lip, were sealed with a cork and a glued on paper label showed details of contents and supplier. It is not unusual to find them with the label still attached. A number of makers used bottles that had their names impressed into the body, but these are rather unusual and any marking is usually only that of the pottery.

Button   Conical   Cotton Reel

Bulk Ink   Blackwood Patent Syphon

One classic impressed example is the "Blackwood Patent Syphon - London", the wording being stamped at the base. It is finished in a grey/ white glaze which is sometimes rather coarse and has an elegant pouring spout. The "syphon" in the name refers to a pump system used to get the ink out, but this is generally missing. The bottle dates around 1885/95 and was probably quite expensive to purchase since bottle diggers seem to find more on better quality sites than on municipal dumps.

There were a few types of stoneware bottles used for "penny inks". Those most often seen are conical, button and cotton reel shapes, usually in saltglaze finish. They were all cork sealed. The conical ink seems to have gone out of production around the turn of the century whilst the other two were still used during the 1920s.

Transfer printed items are very unusual indeed and any that turn up are usually either printing or burnishing inks, rather than a writing ink. Undoubtedly the best transferred item of all is a pot which once held a printing ink with the trade name of "Hectograph." On the front are details of the product, with the trademark of a man in a top hat blowing a posthorn, on the back are detailed instructions for use.

Medicine Bottles

The term Medicines covers the range of preparations and proprietary medicines sold by chemists.

150 years ago there were no health services in the way that we know them today, doctors worked in private practices and charged for their services, their fees often being more than working class families could afford.

The medical profession had yet to find out that bacteria existed and consequently there was no protection against infection. There were no such things as disinfectants or sterile bandages, operations were carried out without the benefit of rubber gloves, operating gowns, masks or sterile instruments and anaesthetics had yet to be invented. The most simple operation often resulted in death by a wound becoming infected and it was not uncommon to report that an operation was a success but the patient had died (meaning that blood poisoning had killed the patient following an operation).

Illnesses such as tuberculosis and consumption were rife and many treatments, now part of everyday life, had yet to be discovered. Antibiotics and immunisation were still a long way off, even the simple Aspirin was seen as something of a wonder drug when it first appeared on the market.

With this sort of medical situation, it is not surprising that home treatments were commonplace. Medicines were often supplied on the local chemist's recommendation, or bought on the strength of newspaper advertisements. The drugs industry was based on preparations of herbs, plants and natural elements, in the early 1800s many chemists grew medicinal plants or collected them from local woods and fields. By the middle of the century, with the expansion of the British Empire, more exotic plants were available from specialist medicinal suppliers who eventually supplied most home grown ingredients as well. At one time medicine was supplied in bottles which held only one individual dose, but by the time Victoria had come to the throne this situation had changed with larger bottles being used. During the latter part of the nineteenth century medicines were often supplied in standard sized bottles with lines embossed on one panel showing the size of the dose to be taken.

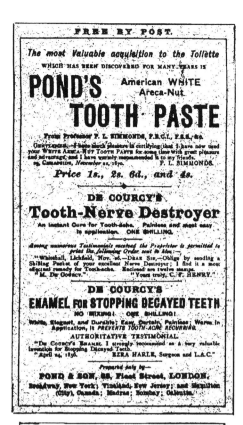

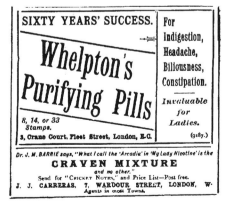

As an added bonus, pre 1900 newspapers and magazines are still quite easy to find and their advertisements give added interest to any collection. The adverts above are from publications between 1880 and 1900.

| Bishops Granular Citrate of caffeine | Galloways Celebrated Cough Syrup | Dark green Boots Cash Chemist | Tricophospherous for the skin & hair |

These lines would often be marked Tablespoons or sometimes Teaspoons and, just as today, the chemist would affix a paper label which gave his name and address together with details of how often the medicine should be taken.

By the late 1900s, the two piece mould had made the cost of bottles cheap enough for even the smallest chemist to market his preparations in bottles with his name and details of the contents embossed on one or more panels. Many chemists supplied the needs of a community in a fairly small area and, with bottle diggers excavating more of the smaller village dumps, it is not surprising that previously unrecorded medicine bottles frequently turn up.

I have repeatedly stated that rarity = high prices, but this is one time when rarity does not equate with value. The range of medicines is so large that collectors either specialise or collect anything local. The result being that a rare item from one area is not given a second look elsewhere and the only known example of a bottle from a village chemist is unlikely to be worth more than a pound or two. Even strong local interest is unlikely to push its price up to much more than double that. Generally the only medicines that command high prices are either coloured examples (especially cobalt blue) or those with unusual or pictorial trademarks

Small chemists faced very stiff competition from a number of large companies such as Allan & Hanbury and Parkes Drug Stores, who provided medicines nationally. The largest range of proprietary medicines was sold by Boots Cash Chemist (today called Boots). The word "cash" was included in the original company name to indicate that the medicine should be paid for at the time of purchase rather than being charged to an account (doubtless there was difficulty in recovering money if the medicine failed to work and the recipient died). There were also a large number of proprietary treatments on the market which relied on newspaper advertising to help keep sales up. The large quantities of bottles for products such as Owbridges Lung Tonic, Eno's Fruit Salts and Elliman's Embrocation which are recovered from Victorian and Edwardian rubbish tips bears testimony to their success.

Embossing on old medicine bottles provides fascinating insight into how people dealt with their ailments. No doubt glycerine and cucumber, extract of herbs or balsam of honey were quite palatable, but linseed compound or cod liver oil with lime and soda must have taken some swallowing. I sometimes get bulk supplies of medicines from some Welsh bottle digging friends. The major industry in their area is (or was) coal mining and the high incidence of mining related lung diseases is underlined by the large quantities of lung tonics and cough cures that they turn up. No doubt bottles from other parts of the country would also show a preponderance of medicines for treating local problems.

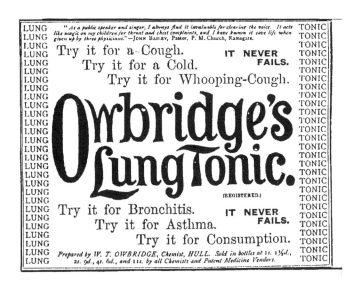

Quack Cures

Quack cures were the fraudulent preparations produced by confidence tricksters. Their express purpose was to take money from a gullible public and sales depended more on the amount of advertising used than on any ability to cure illness. Advertisements generally followed the format that somebody, who was suffering from some illness that had baffled doctors and specialists, had been completely cured by taking one or two bottles of the miracle cure. Claims were often backed by reams of "unsolicited" testimonials.

Few cures contained much that actually helped treat a condition and some were positively dangerous. It was not unusual for them to contain alcohol or opiates which temporarily deadened pain and helped convince sufferers that the condition was improving. Sales were often improved by adding the title of Doctor or the word cure to the product, or by giving it a vague medical name. e.g. Dr. Rookes Solar Elixir; Fennings Fever Curer; Clarkes World Famed Blood Mixture; Dr Kilmers Swamp Root Liver, Bladder and Kidney cure and Dr. Tibbald`s Blood Tonic.

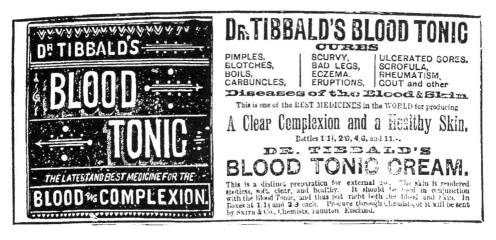

This advert, claiming to cure scurvy, rheumatism and gout, dates from 1883 and is typical of that time.

My favourite quack cure, Mrs Winslow`s Soothing Syrup, was on the market for many years. I have seen one advertisement which claimed that a dying infant had made such a miraculous recovery after taking this "medicine" that it was christened Winslow after the lifesaving cure. However, the sad truth is that it actually contained a small amount of arsenic and was responsible for more deaths than cures. (There was little or no consumer protection in those days.)

In the early 1900s there was a move to stop the trade in quack cures both here and in America. Both proprietary and patent medicines were analysed and the results published, together with a costing of the ingredients. Newspapers had a field day printing details of these concoctions with the result that the market for the majority of the miracle cures disappeared overnight. The contents ranged from "Radnums Microbe Killer" containing 99% water, to an American cure with the most unusual name of "Warners Tippacanoe" which was 99% rum.

Undoubtedly the most outrageous advert of all time must be the one shown below for

Bates Sulphur Salt. It dates from 1882 and claims that by taking the medicine, you could live forever.

Cure for epilepsy and fits

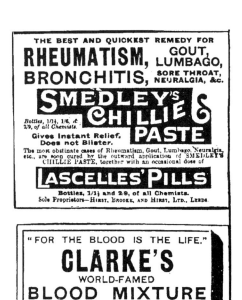

One of the most successful fraudsters was Hubert Harrington Warner. He once worked for a company which manufactured safes and he used this to good effect, calling his products Warner's Safe Cure remedies and using an embossed picture of a safe on wheels as a trademark. Warner was an out and out charlatan but established a successful business in America, spread to Britain, and was eventually selling his products all over the world. His success was the result of prolific and clever advertising. Although his business collapsed when the ingredients of his products were made public around 1906, surprisingly, it was still possible to buy Warner's Safe Cures in Britain right through the 1920s.

Warner's bottles are collected world wide. Although the standard amber half pint and pint bottles have remained at much the same value for a number of years, some of the rarer types such as miniatures, two pint medicines and animal cures have proved to be a good investment with prices rising well over the rate of inflation.

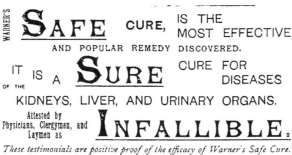

WARNER'S

SAFE CURE, IS THE MOST EFFECTIVE

AND POPULAR REMEDY DISCOVERED.

IT IS A **SURE** CURE FOR DISEASES OF THE

KIDNEYS, LIVER, AND URINARY ORGANS.

Attested by Physicians, Clergymen, and Laymen as **INFALLIBLE.**

These testimonials are positive proof of the efficacy of Warner's Safe Cure.

AN EX-MISSIONARY'S MESSAGE.

"I have for years, since I left India, been a perfect martyr to indigestion, caused by a sluggish liver, and have tried various doctors and their medicines without any permanent benefit. I was induced to try Warner's Safe Cure and Pills, with the result that I am now completely restored to health, and I find by continuing to take one pill at dinner and one dose of Warner's Safe Cure early every morning they keep my digestive organs in good working order.

(Rev.) J. W. Heffenden

"Church House,
"Bordesley Green, Birmingham."

A BURDEN FIFTEEN YEARS.

"For fifteen years my life was a daily burden. I suffered from inflammation of the bladder and indigestion; burning pains in groin and back; excruciating pains in the pit of the stomach; dreadful aching of the eyes; coldness of the extremities; distressing flatulency; pain and burning during urination; and bad taste in the mouth. I was extremely nervous and low-spirited; gradually growing weaker and weaker, with great loss of flesh. After all these years of suffering and fruitless attempts to better my condition, I was cured by Warner's Safe Cure. I can now walk long distances without any pain or inconvenience. Have regained my flesh, and my natural life-vigour has returned, so now I enjoy life and follow my domestic occupations with comfort and ease.

"I do hope this may influence lady sufferers to try this medicine, and shall be pleased to answer any inquiries as to my experience.

(Mrs.) Emily Snell

"40, North Street, Horsham."

A WRONG VERDICT.

"Four years ago I was taken with what seemed a complication of diseases. I suffered frequent attacks of giddiness; could not rest day or night; suffered excruciating pains all over my body, especially severe in the back, below shoulder-blades, sometimes extending to my arms. My appetite was poor, and what little food I ate distressed me. I could not walk, nor even stand upright. I was also tortured by severe pains in my chest and hoarseness, which the club doctor said was due to weakness of the lungs. My local doctor treated me for two years, without effecting amelioration; in fact, after all this time, he said, 'You have kidney disease, and there is no cure for you.'

"I immediately began to take Warner's Safe Cure, and now, I am happy to say, I am completely cured. I owe my life to this medicine, and its merits cannot be too widely known.

J. Long

"Bricklands, Bury Road, Gosport, Hants."

A GRATEFUL LADY.

"Warner's Safe Cure and Warner's Safe Nervine have been the means of restoring me to health after suffering for many years from indigestion, dyspepsia, chronic weakness of the chest, severe headaches, palpitations of the heart, nervous depression, with an occasional attack of bronchitis. Only those who, like myself, have passed through such an unpleasant experience can appreciate a return to good health, and I shall at all times extol the medicines which have done so much for me.

Mrs. W. Ball

"Utkinton Lane, Tarporley, Cheshire."

This popular remedy may be obtained of all Chemists and Dealers at 2/9 and 4/6 per bottle.

Mineral Waters

I can remember a few years ago laughing at the idea of buying bottled water from the supermarket when it came out of the tap for free, but nowadays fizzy water is my preferred beverage when I want a refreshing drink. Although bottled water seems a relatively modern trend, it has been around for well over two centuries.

The health giving properties of naturally mineralised water was being proclaimed by the medical profession as early as mid 1700s. It soon became commonplace for the wealthy to "take the waters" at the spa towns of Bath, Harrogate and Tunbridge Wells, or further afield to Baden Baden and Selters (seltzer water) in Germany. These visits however tended to be as much part of the social scene as for health reasons.

For those who could not afford either the time or expense of such trips, spa water could be purchased from high class shops who sold it in stoneware bottles. At that time the watering places were in private hands and owners were able to charge high prices for their products.

Chemists soon analysed the contents of the water and were able produce passable imitations at a more reasonable cost, although the quality varied. Joseph Priestly perfected a method of putting carbon dioxide into water and his product was used on ships of the Royal Navy from around 1772.

The popularity of carbonised drinks was, to a large extent, due to Joseph Schweppes who started a business in Vienna. He found that water would hold more carbon dioxide if introduced under pressure, he also added compounds such as lithia and magnesia to aid digestive complaints. To make it difficult for his process to be copied he fitted extra pieces to his water treatment machine and had it completely enclosed. Schweppes came to England in 1793, established a business in Bristol and, shortly after, another in London's Drury Lane. In addition to his medicinal waters he also made seltzer waters and still drinks. Mineral water advertising was then based on the premise that the drink was health giving. This resulted in authorities treating it as a medicinal preparation and liable to the tax levied on medicines at that time.

In 1809 William Hamilton patented the first automatic machine for bottling mineral waters making mass production a viable proposition and competition grew as more companies were set up to cater to the public's growing thirst. During the next 25 years, in an effort to gain a larger share of the market, makers flavoured the drink with fruit juices or herbs and sweetened it with sugar or honey.

Surprisingly, it took several years for manufacturers to realise that people were buying the concoctions for their taste rather than for any healthy properties it might contain. In 1833 the medicinal tax was lifted and lower prices helped to raise demand, triggering off a further increase in production with a consequent rise in the number of suppliers. Towards the end of the century every town, as well as many villages, had their own manufacturers supplying, and often oversupplying, local demand.

As competition increased many of the smaller firms were either taken over or forced out of business by their larger competitors who had the finance to support large scale advertising campaigns and price cutting. Eventually the market was dominated by giants such as R. Whites, Rawlings, Batey and, of course, Schweppes. Some of the smaller companies which managed to survive into the 20th century were finally forced to close in the First World War when faced with the problems of trying to produce a luxury product during a time of national shortage.

The first drinks were closed with a cork stopper and hundreds of ideas were tried in an effort to find an alternative way to seal a pressured drink inside a glass bottle. Many designs never made it to the market and others were only produced in small numbers, possibly only being used by one small local firm. In some cases only one or two examples of a particular type of bottle have been found.

The majority of mineral water bottles are found in aqua coloured glass (light sea green), but they also turn up in other colours such as amber, brown, black and various shades of green and blue. Bottles were also produced with an aqua glass body and the lip of another colour, this was not for decoration but served a practical purpose. Since there was a problem with unscrupulous operators pirating and refilling bottles belonging to reputable companies, a coloured lip identified the bottle as belonging to a particular company, even if the name was covered over with a paper label.

Many companies, especially in areas of fierce competition, tried to attract buyers by using highly detailed trademarks covering a wide variety of subjects; animals, transport and buildings being the most common.

It is these ideas, patents, coloured bottles and attractive trade designs which make mineral waters such a popular collecting line.

The value of mineral water bottles varies hugely - a 100 year old bottle from one of the larger firms is usually so common that it may only be worth £1-2, while a similar looking bottle from a previously unrecorded company in an area with a large number of collectors can easily fetch upwards of £50. Some ultra rare bottles (especially the coloured glass variations) have been sold for over £1,000. Despite these abnormally high prices, it is still fairly easy to build up a collection covering a wide variety of types relatively cheaply.

The addition of carbon dioxide into water was a landmark in the history of drinks manufacturing. If it was not for the "fizz" in the drink it is doubtful whether Coca Cola or Pepsi Cola would have such huge international appeal.

The following pages give some background to the more important and revolutionary designs, some of which have stood the test of time and are still in use today.

The Hamilton (also known as a bomb, torpedo or egg)

This bottle is probably named after somebody who did not invent it. The confusion is caused by the patent that William Hamilton took out on his bottle filling machine in 1809. One diagram showed this type of bottle as being suitable for use on his machine and, for this reason, he has been credited with its design. However, it is probable that Schweppes was already using it for his beverages at least 15 years earlier.

The bottle was sealed with a tight fitting cork and this was further secured by tying it in place with wire or string. The pointed base ensured that the bottle was stored laying on its side so that the contents kept the cork wet and prevented it from drying out and shrinking (in the same way that corked wine bottles are stored on their sides).

This type of bottle was used for about 100 years, the early examples were free blown and later versions made in two piece moulds. In 1893 a variation was patented with a flat bottom, this too was stored on its side but could be stood upright when used.

Barrett and Eler patent

It is strange that, with Victorian businessmen being so adapt at finding business opportunities, it was over 60 years before a new design for mineral water bottles was marketed. In 1864 John Joseph came up with an idea for sealing bottles by using a ball forced into its neck. Four years later an adaptation of this design was patented by Barratt and Eler. They used a wooden stick fitted with a washer rather than a ball. The internal gas pressure of the drink forced the stick into the bottle's neck, the washer forming an airtight seal.

To open the drink it was simply a matter of pushing down the stick to release the gas pressure. The washer was heavy enough to make the stick sink and prevent it from interfering with pouring out the drink.

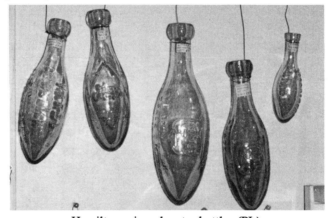

Hamilton mineral water bottles (PL)

Flat bottom Hamilton   Barrett and Eler

Although the Barratt and Eler design had only limited success, it did trigger off other inventors who came up with porcelain stoppers, wired on caps and even a crude attempt at a crown cap. Then, on the 24 November 1870, Hiram Codd was granted patent No. 3070 for a revolutionary idea using a glass marble as a seal. He improved on the basic design, taking out two further patents, and in 1872 the "Codd" bottle was born.

The drink contained much more carbon dioxide than we see today. When the bottle was filled there was enough pressure to keep the marble pressed tightly against a rubber washer in the neck making an airtight seal.

To open the bottle it was only necessary to push down the marble and release the gas pressure. The lugs in the neck were to trap the marble when the drink was poured.

The bottle was hand blown into a 2 piece mould and the blowing rod broken away to leave a jagged top, once the bottle was cool the marble was put in. The final step was to add more glass to the lip of the bottle and shape the top.

Codd's bottle was an immediate success, in 1873 it won medals at the London and Vienna exhibitions and it was not long before orders were coming in from all over the world.

Hiram Codd was primarily an inventor and went into partnership with Dan Rylands who already had an established glass-making company. Codd and Rylands both patented improvements on the design, many were variations on the lugs trapping the marble although one ingenious idea had a glass valve for releasing the gas pressure.

Although the Codd/Rylands company was highly successful, the two men did not get on very well. This was not helped by Rylands taking out his own patents and making improvements to the special glass making tools Codd had invented. In 1884 the acrimonious partnership was dissolved with Codd selling out to Rylands.

The bottles were extremely popular but they had a number of problems: their life was often short with children breaking them to get out the marbles and when they were returned for refilling it was a time consuming and awkward job to clean them (as any bottle digger can testify). Also, they were not very hygienic as dirt tended to lie in the recess above the marble.

Hiram Codd was still coming up with ideas despite his split with Dan Rylands and in 1886 he patented the idea of having the type of product printed on the ring in the neck of the bottle. Unfortunately his inventive genius was lost with his death in 1887.

The Codd bottle was a breakthrough in design and others were not slow to patent their own variations to get a share of the profits associated with the bottle.

The Hybrid

This is quite a scarce item which combines both the Codd and the Hamilton bottles. There are many theories concerning the reason for this design. I personally think that some of the smaller glassworks just adapted their Hamilton moulds rather than going to the expense of replacing them.

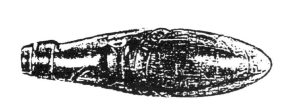

Hybrid   Valve Codd

Over 500 patents were taken out relating to bottle closures in the period 1870 to 1900. Some were entirely new inventions, such as the Edward's patent which is basically a flat bottomed Hamilton, but with a projecting groove running round near the base which trapped the stopper.

Many patents were granted for ideas which were only minor alterations to the Codd bottle. Codd variations include the Connors patent which had a pear shaped stopper; Shaw's patent was a standard bottle with ribbing on the neck for added strength; Haynes' used an elongated stopper and Mills used a ribbed (beehive) top to protect the lip.

Other variations that turn up occasionally are the Sykes/Mackvay patent which has six dimples just above the base, whilst other types have only four dimples. Few Codd variants had any real success, many were never actually produced, some had only very localised outlets, whilst there was no room for others in an already saturated market. The best example of not finding a niche in the market was the Hutchinson stopper patented by Lake in 1883. His invention did not catch on in Britain but it became extremely popular when introduced to the American market.

One idea that did become successful was the Bullet Stopper. The name stems from the shape of the stopper but, in reality, the bottle was an update of Barrett and Eler's design. The first patent for a bullet stopper (No. 1923) was taken out by John Lamont on 2nd June 1874 and covered both the shape of the bottle and its stopper. In 1860 he took out another patent with the stopper having a hollowed out base so that the weight of the top would help seat it more easily into the bottle. Early examples were embossed on the rear "Lamont's Patent" and a hand holding a bottle as a trademark.

Internal screw thread

Although bottles with an efficient outside thread could not be produced until advent of bottle making machines, it was possible to produce a crude thread cut inside the lip. The bottle was sealed by means of a rubber washer mounted on a threaded stopper made from a hard wood, lignum vitae which was later replaced by a hard rubber compound called Vulcanite. The thread was just a couple of twists in the glass but it gave sufficient grip to screw the stopper in enough to flatten the washer and provide an effective seal.

Although the design was patented by Henry Barrett in 1871, it was several years before the bottle came into use. Barrett supplied bottled mineral water and many of his bottles, together with their stoppers, had embossing on them to advertise this closure (even bottles still sealed with a cork).

Most stoppers had the supplier's name cut into them. When charging bottle deposits were used, it was necessary to return the correct stopper with a bottle to get the refund. From the collecting point of view, this type of bottle looks incomplete when the stopper is missing. It can be almost impossible to find one bearing the correct name but, since the thread was more or less standardised throughout the trade, the tops are interchangeable and one of the unmarked tops which appeared around 1930 can be fitted.

The thin flat top gave a poor grip which could make opening the bottle difficult. In 1885 Riley patented a variation with a chisel shaped top which used a slotted bar to give additional leverage, these stoppers generally carry the words "Riley Patent". Another variety was patented by Higson in 1903 which had a hole drilled through it and used a piece of stiff wire to give a better grip.

The Internal Screw Thread was found to be the perfect seal for beer bottles and was used extensively in the brewing industry. Its simplicity impressed mineral water manufacturers and by 1900 it had largely replaced the Codd. The seal was still in use in the 1950s, although by this time it was being replaced by the crown cap which was cheaper to produce

Swing Stopper

Several inventors tried to secure caps with wire but their ideas were largely unsuccessful. One of the main problems was that the wire used was of poor quality and easily rusted. This drawback was solved with the coming of galvanised wire.

In 1875 an ingenious design, called the lighning or swing stopper was patented by Charles De Quillfeldt. He used a porcelain stopper with a ring of rubber fitted to a projection on the bottom and two pieces of wire linked together in such a way that it was possible to lever the stopper in and out of the top of the bottle. It was over 30 years before the seal caught on in Britain, despite having proved itself in the USA. The bottle was used for mineral waters, stone ginger beers (more commonly in Scotland) and a few dairies used the idea to seal milk bottles. Today the closure is enjoying a mini revival with a few breweries such as Grolsch and The Newquay Steam Brewery who use it as a sales gimmick.

Swing stopper

The Crown Cap

In 1892 William Painter invented a closure using a disposable metal cap as a seal. A recess was cut around the lip of the bottle to take a cork lined metal cap shaped to grip the recess. Since the cap was discarded when the bottle was opened, it saved on the cost of replacing or cleaning the internal screw stoppers. These bottles were first made in two piece moulds but they were not very popular as it was difficult to hand cut the recess yet keep the lip strong enough to prevent it breaking when the cap was levered off.

With the arrival of the bottle making machine it became possible for manufacturers to produce bottles to a very high standard, each one being precisely the same as the previous one. Machines were

developed to both fill and seal the bottles and gradually the crown cap started to replace other closures until it became indispensable to the soft drinks and brewing industries. Production reached its peak after the Second World War and it is still used today.

Many suppliers gave away bottle openers carrying their company name. These are still very easy to find, usually costing only a few pence to buy, they can make interesting and cheap additions to a collection, or even a collection by themselves.

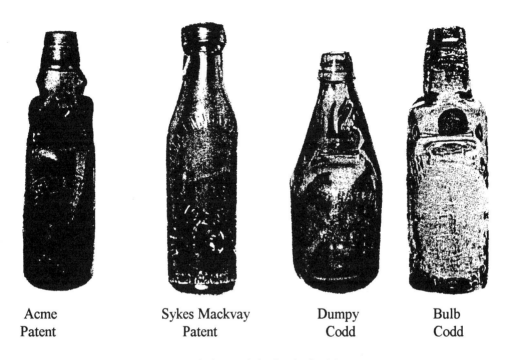

| Acme | Sykes Mackvay | Dumpy | Bulb |
| Patent | Patent | Codd | Codd |

Variations of the basic Codd

Beer Bottles

During the 18th and early 19th centuries a small amount of bottled beer was available. Some was even being exported to the British colonies, although at that time it was an expensive commodity which could only be afforded by the rich. If working class families wanted to drink beer at home they took a jug to the local pub and had it filled over the counter.

In those days beer bottles did not exist and the drink was supplied in the same bottles as those used for wine, having a paper label stuck on to identify the contents. The reason that beers from this age are impossible to identify is that once the label has gone then the bottle itself looks like an ordinary wine bottle.

During the latter half of the 18th century there were a number of breweries around who had their own outlets, but much of the beer sold in hostelries was home brewed on the premises. The situation changed in the 1800s when pubs were supplied by one of thousands of breweries. These ranged from national suppliers such as Whitbread who had outlets all over the country, to small firms whose output was only sufficient to supply their local village.

Beer was a part of everyday working life. One of the reasons it was so popular was that water was often contaminated, with beer the water is boiled during the brewing process making it safer to drink than water (despite the side effect of drunkenness). In 1870 the average annual consumption was 34 gallons for every man, woman and child in the country.

Glass bottles specifically designed to hold beer did not make an appearance on the British market until around 1870 when cheap two and three piece moulds arrived on the scene. It then became possible to mass produce bottles to a fairly consistent size, some early mould blown beers have the words "Imperial Pint" or "Imperial Half Pint" embossed on the shoulder.

The bottles are usually a dark green colour, sometimes so dark that the glass appears to be black. The dark colour helped to prolong the life of the contents and also prevented customers seeing any unsightly residue in the drink. Bottles are most commonly found in half pint and pint sizes but large quart (two pint) bottles occasionally turn up.

Towards the end of the century it was possible to have supplier's details embossed on to the surface of the bottle. Some brewers tried to attract customers by using elaborately detailed trademarks or even a spurious coat of arms in the hope that the buyer would assume Royal patronage. A paper label showing the actual contents or particular brew was also stuck to the bottle.

The cost of embossing was just a few pence per gross, little more than having to replace a couple of bottles. The great advantage was that it denoted ownership and empty bottles were more likely to be returned to the brewery for refilling.

The earliest beer bottles were sealed with corks, sometimes having them tied into place with wire or string for added security. The next stage was the internal screw thread and when machine made bottles came on the scene there was a gradual move to the crown cap. The only other closure which turns up with any regularity is the swing stopper.

Not all beer bottles were made in glass, some stoneware porter bottles were in use from the early 1800s. These were usually finished in a slip glaze with the brewers name stamped (or impressed) into the clay before being fired in the kiln. Most of these bottles come from the North of England. They do not turn up very often, tending to end up in local collections. These can be relatively expensive. Prices start at about £25 for a common item and can run up to over £100.

There are also some stoneware flagons, the most common sizes held either half or one gallon but they also turn up in larger capacities. Flagons (originally called jars) used specifically for beer can be quite hard to track down as these containers were used for many other products. Early examples carry impressed details and were found both in slip glaze and a much more appealing saltglaze finish. When transfer printing arrived some brewers added attractive pictorial trademarks. Most embossed flagons are in the £10 - £20 price range, but a transfer printed example in perfect condition with a good trademark can cost well over £50.

It would take a small warehouse to display a complete range of beer bottles. In the late 1800s there were so many breweries around that 100 year old embossed beer bottles can be picked up for a pound or two. Bottles carrying an interesting pictorial trade mark may cost five times that. The only glass beer bottles which command any sort of price are either exceptional examples (usually in black glass) which carry a superbly detailed or unusual trademark, scarce items from an area with a large number of local collectors or those using an unusual closure.

Old beers which still have their labels still intact are collected by some, as are the modern commemorative bottles such as those issued for the Royal wedding or to mark a significant point in the brewery's history. Prices reflect the limited numbers in circulation and the value is increased if the bottle is full.

As with mineral water suppliers, many breweries gave away metal bottle openers for levering off crown caps - usually these have the brewers' name stamped on it as a bit of cheap advertising. These can often be found for a few pence - another collecting line?

Baby Feeders

Today's plastic baby feeding bottles are rarely given a second look but their history can be traced back over 2,000 years. In Roman times infants were fed from glass or stoneware feeding bottles. Cows horns were used in the middle ages, leather or wooden feeders during the reign of the first Queen Elizabeth and pewter "suckling bottles" were employed in the 17th and 18th centuries.

Around 1830 feeders were being made from white china, known as Boat feeders after the shape, one end being pointed and the other end flat. Some were highly decorated with flowers, patterns or scenes (usually in blue and white). These are much sought after today, prices are well over the £100 mark and a lot more if made by a recognised pottery such as Davenport, Copeland, Spode or Wedgwood.

Early Victorian china feeders

The increased call for labour caused by the industrial revolution gave rise to more women going to work and led to a demand for baby feeding bottles for child minders to care for infants while mothers worked. By the middle of the 19th century glass feeders were being made but were very expensive, adverts from the time show prices to be around seven shillings. Increased demand brought more manufacturers on the scene, the added competition, especially from France, and the use of moulds helped drastically reduce prices to around one shilling. The Cow & Gate advertisement shown overleaf dates from 1916 and shows the price was still only two shillings or less.

The use of the right tradename played its part in determining sales and suppliers took full advantage of the ability to emboss bottles, a clever use of a name was the popular "Hygienic" feeder. Some used an implied royal connection to help sales, such as the "Alexandra" and the "Victoria" bottles, others using names designed to appeal to the mothering instinct, e.g. "Little Rosebud" and "Our Little Darling".

The business end of the bottle was fitted with a teat made from a variety of materials, usually rag or wash leather, but sometimes lambs or calves teats were used, having been recycled by slaughterhouses and pickled in brine. In 1845 india rubber teats became available helping to change in bottle design and reduce the high infant mortality rate.

Early Victorian feeders had the teat fitted on the end. With the arrival of the rubber teat this shape became rounded with a flat back and an offset neck, this used a rubber tube with a teat moulded on one end and the tube being held in place by a threaded glass stopper. The major drawback with this type of bottle was the near impossible task of cleaning the tube which harboured bacteria and led to huge numbers of baby deaths caused by gastric disorders. The medical profession nicknamed it the "Murder" bottle and, despite its appalling reputation, it was still possible to purchase this type of feeder until the 1920s. During the 1890s some American States banned its use and many bottles were then shipped to Britain where no such ban operated. Feeders such as the "Alabama" and "Picanniny" are not uncommon here.

By 1900 an improved bottle had been marketed with the teat fitting directly on to the bottle, but it did not prove popular as the hygienic and easy to clean "Banana" shaped feeder had arrived on the scene. The bottle was open at both ends, one of which took a teat, the other had a rubber cap with a small hole in which allowed air to enter the bottle and enabled the contents to be drunk without a vacuum forming. This made feeding much easier as the baby swallowed less air with the milk and required less patting to get rid of excess air after a feed.

Glass boat shape c1830

Maws Alexandra feeder c1880

Pocock patent with integral
thermometer c1885

Collecting baby feeders is one line where it is only necessary to have a few bottles to cover all the major designs, most varieties are little more than variations on the basic shape. A display can be added to with tiny copies of the various bottles which were used by girls to feed their dolls, or with associated embossed bottles. Common examples are Woodwood's gripe water (early bottles are blue, later versions are aqua and later still clear glass); Mellins infant food jars (in two sizes); Pritchards teething powders (there are several varieties of this small bottle and it is worth looking for the sheared top variety in which the "R" in Try reversed). There are also a number of infants and children's medicine and shampoo bottles to be found.

Poison Bottles

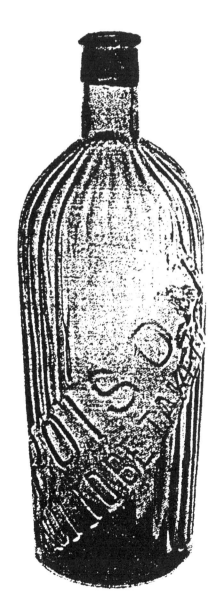

These bottles once contained toxic substances such as embrocation, acid, disinfectant or even ear or eye drops. Over a century ago, before consumer protection laws appeared on the statute books, several poisonous substances were freely available. Dangerous chemicals such as Carbolic Acid (often used as a disinfectant) and rat poisons were commonly found in homes. Many cases of death by poisoning (accidental or otherwise) were recorded every year, especially amongst children.

In 1829, New York State passed a law in which poisonous substances had to be clearly marked with the word POISON on their containers. This idea was put to the British parliament in 1847, but it was decided that packaging arrangements should be to suppliers and chemists. A further bill was also defeated in 1863, but this gave birth to a flood of ideas and inventions to improve safety.

One idea that was almost universally adopted was the use of coloured bottles. Most poisons were made in green, blue or brown glass, their distinctive colouring gave a visual warning to a population in which illiteracy was commonplace.

Supplying poisons in coloured glass containers was not sufficient safeguard in itself and it is quite possible that children may have been attracted by the brightly coloured bottles, despite being given parental warnings.

Today when it gets dark we just turn on a light. Lighting in Victorian homes was generally quite dismal with a choice between candles or oil lamps (gas lighting was available in most large towns, but only to those who could afford it). In many homes lighting was often insufficient to distinguish colours, so the bottle's shape became an important safety factor, being designed to be recognised by touch.

A number of novel ideas were patented in an attempt to produce safe containers. Complicated devices were used to secure stoppers, one had a sealed top and the opening in the base, some were connected to bells which rang when bottle was moved and one design had a bell fitted into the hollowed out stopper. One inventor had a label made from treated paper which glowed in the dark and whilst another label idea was to use glasspaper or sandpaper.

Although a few bottles were produced shaped in the form of skulls or coffins, some more practical and simple designs which came into general use. One common factor was to use heavily embossed ribs or pimples to assist recognition, especially in the dark.

The most common shape found is a six sided bottle with ribbing along the full length of three adjacent panels, often the words NOT TO BE TAKEN was also embossed on the front panel. This design was invented by of William Barker and John Savory, in 1859 it became the first poison bottle to be patented in Britain.

One rather nice variety of this design is a Scottish bottle with a neck almost as long as its body. It has a burst lip and comes in three or four sizes and is usually made in a blue glass which is so deep in colour that it is difficult to tell if the bottle is empty.

The six sided poison was most commonly made in green or cobalt blue, but it can be found in shades of brown and later bottles turn up in clear glass. Early bottles are known with sheared tops.

Almost as common is a rectangular shape with heavy ribbing down the front and two sides. This also carries the legend NOT TO BE TAKEN on the front panel. Both this and the six sided shapes are found in a range of sizes, usually between one and eight ounces, although they can go up to over 20 ounces. Sometimes the capacity can be found on the base and both types are also found bearing the word POISONOUS or POISON.

There are variations, some are plain on all four panels, but these probably would not have held poison.

These are found in the same colours as six sided poisons and again, some of the early examples come with sheared tops.

Probably the third most common shape is triangular, called the "Practical Poison Bottle" it was a Lewis and Towers patent. This has a plain back and rows of diamond shaped pimples embossed on its sides, its narrow front panel is just wide enough to carry the "NOT TO BE TAKEN" warning.

The early examples carry a registration number 334871 on the back which shows the design date as 1899. It is found in a wide range of sizes, the capacity may be marked on the base. This comes in blue, green and occasionally brown glass.

Lysol disinfectant bottles appeared in the early 1900s and these can be looked at as a possible collecting line in their own right. Although the shape tends to stay the same, they do vary in size and can be found in greens and blues as well as the standard brown or amber. A square sectioned variety with the trade name Toxol can also found in a wide range of sizes.

There are a number of other shapes which turn up fairly regularly, such as a triangular one with a rounded back (Hobnail poison) or round bottles carrying the word POISON or POISONOUS. Other designs should be seen as being at least unusual and possibly rare and some poisons are seen by collectors as being among the top 20 most desirable bottles.

After the turn of the century there was a move towards the more general use of aqua glass poison bottles, but still using embossed ribbing, the words POISON or POISONOUS are rather more common.

Desirability, rarity and a reluctance of owners to part with their treasures has helped push up values of rare poisons. One example is the Eclipse patent (No. 6234 - 29th March 1894), this is better known as the Wasp Waist poison and the invention of W. Stephenson. A classic British bottle which has proved to be an investment item. In 1977 it was valued at £15-20, 1987 saw it fetching around £200 and 1997 saw one sell at auction for £1,150.

Another ultra rare bottle is the O'Reilly Patent (Binocular poison) of 1905. This tiny bottle has a groove running from base to middle on the front and another running the full length of the back.

A set of three sizes of skull shaped poison bottles was auctioned for £5,700. But the record price paid at auction was set in 1997 for a coffin shaped bottle (patent No. 5058) which went for £6,700.

Other rarities, although not quite reaching the above levels, can still fetch several hundred pounds and there seems to be no shortage of buyers. Bottles falling into this category include the peculiarly shaped cobalt blue Submarine which is found in three sizes, the little wedge shaped Quine's patent (1893) in clear glass and Martin's Patent of 1902 which was designed to lie on its back, a "U" bend in the neck prevented spillage.

Submarine   Quine's patent

Of course three and four figure sums are only paid for extremely rare items. Although it would be a very expensive business to start a major collection today, a wide variety of shapes and sizes are available. Combined with the bright colours, this means that an attractive display can be put together fairly easily with a minimum number of bottles, especially when positioned in front of a window or to make use of available lighting.

Stoneware Poisons

Very few stoneware poison bottles were produced and most have transfer printing. The commonest bottles were those used by Plynine, a Scottish company who supplied household ammonia. A number of sizes and variations are known, including one which advises the using a tablespoon full for an invigorating bath.

This company also supplied the same product in a giant bottle with the tradename "JUMBOMONIA" which advises that the grocer would refund sixpence for an empty container, but it was worth more if kept for use as a hot water bottle.

There were several other ammonia suppliers using printed stoneware bottles, the most attractive is probably Inman's who used an eagle as a trademark and whose bottle had a honey coloured neck.

Other types of printed stone pots are known for arsenate of lead but these are quite rare and hard to track down. Rather easier to find are the pots which once held mercury, especially in the smaller sizes. They are usually plain but printed examples are found occasionally. I have a transfer printed example in the shape of a miniature flagon.

Impressed stoneware pots are very unusual and the only type which seems to appear regularly is a small white glazed item of similar shape to a furniture polish jar. It is impressed "Poison" just below the shoulder and Royal Infirmary Manchester near the base.

It was also possible to purchase poison in bulk supplied in flagons with horizontal ribbing and sky blue glazed finish on the shoulder and lip, the word POISON was printed on the shoulder. These containers are unusual or rare.

Soda Syphons

Over the years drinking fashions change. Today's "in" drinks seem to be obscure lagers drunk straight from the bottle, a few years ago the lady's tipple was rum with blackcurrant juice or port and lemonade and at one time whisky was usually diluted with soda water. This was free and dispensed from syphons found on the bars of public houses where whisky drinkers could help themselves. Sometimes syphons were kept on a stand or a dish which advertised the company supplying the soda water. These are quite scarce and are eagerly sought after by collectors of advertising, soda syphons and mineral water items.

It is uncertain who invented the soda syphon and credit is divided between Charles Plinth who invented a "portable fountain" in 1813 and John Nooth who produced a Gazogene for aerating water around 1775. Certainly May and Co. were advertising one made from porcelain in the mid 1800s and it is likely that cylindrical shaped glass examples were introduced to England after being shown at the 1867 Paris Exhibition. The first cylindrical syphons were French made but the home market was eventually dominated by the London Syphon Company.

Early syphons, called Seltzogenes, were nearly two feet tall and consisted of two joined globes, one above the other. The bottom was filled with water and the upper with bicarbonate of soda and tartaric acid, the contents of the two globes two being kept apart by means of a stopper. When the stopper was removed the elements mixed with the water causing effervescence which built up sufficient pressure to force the soda water out through a spout when a handle was depressed to release a valve in the neck.

French advertisement showing three different types of syphon.

Although Seltzogenes had very thick walls made from good quality glass, the gas pressure was sometimes strong enough to make the bottle explode. To reduce the risk of injury they were covered in fine wire mesh or woven cane.

Towards the end of the nineteenth century the cylindrical shape so loved by early comedy film makers came into being. Although the method of pressurising the contents has altered, this shape has remained much the same.

The first cylindrical syphons were factory filled through a screw fitting under a cap in the top and the soda water was introduced into the syphon under pressure. The top contains a spring loaded valve operated by a lever, when the valve is opened gas pressure forces the liquid up a glass tube and out through a spout.

Metal topped syphons are almost impossible to date with any degree of accuracy. The only clues are the shape of the spout, the method of fixing the operating handle (earlier ones are often secured by a small screw and a nut) and the material the top is made from. The first tops were made from pewter or tin, followed by chrome plating and finally plastic. More modern examples are pressurised with a "Sparklets" bulb and the first of these were encased in metal mesh which is sometimes chrome plated (Sparklets types are probably a future collecting line).

It is not unusual to find syphons where the name in the glass is different to that stamped into the metal top. I once had one from a cellar where not only did the two names not match, but the paper neck label was from a third company. The reason for this is that most soda water suppliers contracted out the filling process and when the syphons were stripped down for cleaning the tops could be mixed up.

Soda syphons are generally made in clear glass with the supplier's name acid etched into the surface, although basically cylindrical in shape there are variations such as having tapered sides. Some have heavy fluting down their length, others are quite plain and a few have faceted panels, there are even miniature versions although these are rather more unusual. Occasionally syphons can be found in a variety of colours. Blue glass is the most common followed by green, amber, pink, yellow and red.

A word of warning - a few years ago there were a large number of syphons around which were painted in various colours and some of these occasionally reappear on the market. They are fairly easy to spot when the paint is on the outside as it can be scratched with a thumbnail. It is much harder to tell when paint has been applied to the inside of the glass. The only way to identify these is to look through the very base to see whether this is clear or coloured glass.

In Britain syphons were usually only found in public houses or the homes of the more wealthy. This was somewhat different to America where soda water was a popular as a drink in its own right. Many cities had soda roundsmen (rather like our milkmen) who made deliveries to homes. The first bottle was bought and paid for, but the customer only paid for the contents when an empty syphon was exchanged for a filled one.

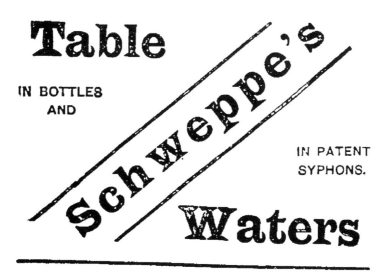

AS SUPPLIED TO THE QUEEN.

Table

IN BOTTLES AND

Schweppe's

IN PATENT SYPHONS.

Waters

Victorian ink bottles (PL)

Ginger beer bottles (PL)

Both photos are part of the author's stock at his bottle stall in the Horse Hospital at
Camden's Stables Market

Chapter 4: Stoneware

Stoneware

In the bottle collecting world, the term stoneware is normally used as a collective term for containers made from clay. However, true stoneware is a mixture of clay and sand or crushed flint fired at a very high temperature (1,200 - 1,300 degrees C).

The popularity of certain jars can be seen when digging for bottles on Victorian tips. Huge quantities of marmalade and jam pots are found and reddish-brown cream pots, together with white jars, which once held polish, sometimes also turn up in abundance. These items were given a quick coat of white or brown glaze before firing, but generally glazed items appear more often from the early 1900s when packaging started to play a more important part in determining sales.

Saltglaze

As with the bottle making industry, competition was fierce and low prices were necessary for a business to survive. To help keep costs down, potteries used the cheapest production methods available. Not surprisingly saltglaze was very popular finish as it was a relatively cheap and simple operation that involved little more than shovelling salt into the kiln at its peak firing temperature. The salt burnt off into a gas which coated the pots in a hard wearing non porous finish which is unaffected by boiling water or most acids. Liquid glaze gave a fairly even colouring whereas the texture and colour of saltglaze depended on a number of factors including the amount and grade of salt used and where an item stood in the kiln. Jars are often dark brown on one side and almost white on the other.

NONPAREIL DE GUICHE
Parisian Polish
(For Varnishing Dress Boots and Shoes)
is more elastic and easier to use than any other.

MELTONIAN BLACKING
(As used in the Royal Household)

Although the technique of saltglazing has been known for over 800 years, it really came into its own in the Victorian era. The first recorded use of the method in Britain was by the Fulham Pottery which was established in the early 1670s. The owner, John Dwight, took out a patent for manufacturing saltglaze, this had expired by 1700 and other companies were quick to copy the process. The increase in demand for packaging during the 1800s saw many new potteries opening up to cater for an expanding market. Some of these are household names today.

The largest supplier of the day was Bourne of Denby, the company was established by Joseph Bourne in 1805. Towards the end of the century the pottery was turning out thousands of bottles every week. The little impressed oval trademark carrying the words "BOURNE DENBY" is well known to bottle buffs.

Almost as important were James Stiff of Lambeth (est.1840), Lovatt and Lovatt, Price of Bristol, Port Dundas (Glasgow) and Edinburgh's Portobello pottery. There were hundreds of other potteries around the country, some of whom just supplied the needs of local industry and may be common in one area but almost unheard of elsewhere.

The best known company of all is probably that set up in Lambeth by John Doulton and John Watts in 1815. They soon built a reputation for high quality whilst making everyday items such as ginger beer and ink bottles, blacking pots as well as water and sewage pipes. The company is today called Royal Doulton and better known around the world for its highly collectable figures and quality tableware.

The oldest saltglazed items in bottle collecting are Bellarmine jugs (referred to as Cologne ware in antique circles) in which wine, and maybe beer, was imported from Cologne and Frenchen (the Rhineland) towards the end of the sixteenth century. The bottles usually carry a bearded face on the shoulder and neck which represents Cardinal Robert Bellarmino who was hated for his preaching against alcohol whilst being a drinker himself. Some also carry a coat of arms, and these, together with smaller sized jugs are more highly rated. Some Bellarmines were produced by English potteries during Victoria's reign which could be confused with earlier examples, although the glazing of later items is usually of far better quality.

Another collecting line in early stoneware is that of pub flasks and flagons which come in a number of different finishes: slip glazed in which the glazing is just a coat of watered down clay, (usually a sign of an early item), two toned where the shoulder and top are in a different colour to the body and saltglazed. Some carry the name and address of a publican, a brewer or wine merchant stamped into the body or shoulder. Although the correct term for this is incising they are usually referred to as being impressed. The most collectable items are those in which the suppliers' details were stamped into to a slab of clay which was then stuck to the shoulder of the piece. This type of bottle is known as a slab seal.

Some saltglazed pieces are decorated with figures or animals made separately and stuck to the body of the piece prior to firing in the kiln. The decoration is normally called sprigging. The commonest examples of these are the "Harvest" jugs which come in several sizes and carry a hunting or rustic scene. Normally people look at the base to see if they carry a Doulton mark, but unmarked examples can carry much better decoration. Sometimes jugs were made for certain customers and may carry their name and even a date. (I have one impressed "E. SALES 1902" but cannot trace any details.)

Reform Flasks are a highly sought after category in saltglazing. They were novelty pieces used to help sell spirits and first appeared in the early 1820s. The bottles either recognised famous people of the day or commemorated special events such as the opening of the Thames tunnel in 1843. Some were made in the shape of a person, others were standard shaped flasks carrying relief mouldings.

In 1832 the first Reform bill was introduced by Lords Russell, Grey and Brougham. This Act of Parliament was a popular move giving voting rights to a larger part of the population. Naturally the proposers of the bill became subjects for these bottles and it is this bill which gives this type of spirit flask its name.

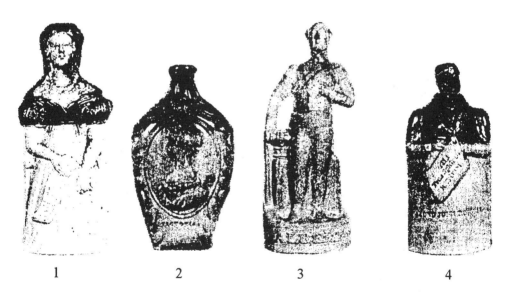

1   2   3   4

1. Queen Victoria, scroll reads "May peace and prosperity prevail"
2. Queen Victoria, shows Duchess of Kent on REVERSE
3. Prince Albert
4. Lord John Russell, scroll reads "The true spirit of reform"
   (a play on words for the spirit contained in the flask).

Royal figures were represented by Queen Victoria, King George IV and his wife Queen Caroline and other famous figures included military leaders such as the Duke of

Wellington and politicians, such as the Prime Minister Lord Melbourne. There was even a flask in the form of a famous music hall comic - Jim Crow.

Although the mid 1850s saw the end of the reform flask era, the idea did not completely die off and small numbers were produced right up until 1910 when Doulton made a set of political figures.

Reform flasks were finished both in saltglaze and a dark chocolate brown colouring called treacle glaze, the latter is less highly rated than saltglaze examples and thus cheaper. During the past decade or so there has been recognition of the historical significance of reform flasks and they have become recognised as antiques, with a corresponding increase in value. Fairly common items can easily fetch upwards of £200.

Saltglazed bottles were made in their thousands, the majority being used for packaging everyday liquid household goods such as black lead, polishes, inks and ginger beer. The huge quantities made means that large numbers are available which has helped to keep prices down. A good assortment of shapes and sizes can still be picked up for just a pound or two each. Commemorative or decorative items are much harder to find and their scarcity is generally reflected in the asking price, often into three figures.

By the early 1900s transfer printing started to replace saltglazing and this, in its turn, was largely phased out by the 1930s. Odd pieces were still being produced much later and I have a flagon with several lines of writing which is dated 1964.

Saltglaze is a superb material that gives a room, or a corner, a rustic feel, it works extremely well with dried flowers or grasses. Being nonporous means that it can also be used for cut flowers - my wife and I raid the stock every spring for blacking jars to use as vases for the daffodils we both like so much.

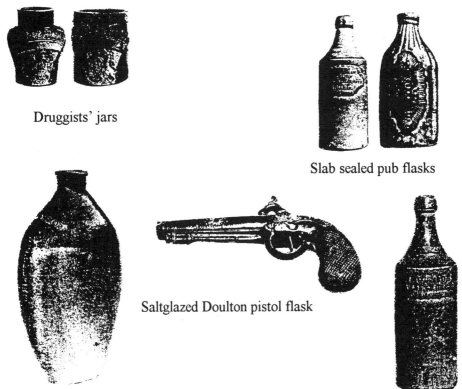

Druggists' jars

Slab sealed pub flasks

Saltglazed Doulton pistol flask

Impressed pub flask lozenge shape

Slab sealed Porter

ALE, GINGER BEER, INK & BLACKING BOTTLES, &c.

ALE, PORTER & GINGER BEER BOTTLES.

ALE BOTTLE. PORTER BOTTLE. GINGER BEER BOTTLE.

	Qts.	6 to Gal.	Pts.	12 to Gal	½-pt, Ales.	½-pt. Gingers.
	30s.	20s.	18s.	14s.	12s. 6d.	11s. per Gross.

INK BOTTLES.

1-oz.	2-oz.	3-oz.	4-oz.	5-oz.	6 oz.
4s.	5s.	6s. 6d.	7s. 6d.	8s.	9s.
8-oz.	10-oz.	12-oz.	16-oz.	20-oz.	
10s. 6d.	12s.	13s.	16s.	18s.	
24-oz.	32-oz.	36-oz.	40-oz.		
24s.	27s.	28s. 6d.	30s. per gross.		

INK BOTTLES, SPOUTED.

1-oz.	2-oz.	3-oz.	4-oz.	5-oz.	6-oz.
5s.	6s.	7s. 6d.	8s. 6d.	9s.	10s.
8-oz.	10 oz.	12-oz.	16-oz.	20-oz.	24 oz.
11s. 6d.	13s.	16s.	18s.	20s.	26s.
32-oz.		36-oz.		40-oz.	
29s.		30s. 6d.		32s. per gross.	

DWARF INKS.

1-oz.	1½-oz.	2 oz.
2s. 6d.	3s.	3s. 6d. per gross.

INKSTANDS.

4s. 6d. per dozen.

TALL. LOW.

BLACKING AND POLISH BOTTLES.

	¼-pt.	½-pt.	1s. size.	1s. 6d. size.
	8s.	11s.	13s. 6d.	17s. per gross.
White Glazed,	9s.	12s.	16s.	19s. ,,

BRUNSWICK BLACK BOTTLES.

¼-pt.	½-pt.	1-pt.
8s.	12s.	20s. per gross.

QUICKSILVER BOTTLES.

½-lb.	1-lb.	2-lb.	3-lb.	4 lb	6-lb.
10d.	1s.	1s. 3d.	1s. 9d.	2s.	2s. 3d.
7-lb.	8-lb.	10-lb.	12-lb.	14-lb.	28-lb.
2s. 6d.	2s. 9d.	3s. 3d.	3s. 9d	4s. 4d.	5s. 6d. doz.

SCENT BOTTLES.

½-oz.	1-oz.	2-oz.
12s.	14s.	17s. per gross.

BELLIED. UPRIGHT.

ANNATTO BOTTLES.

2½-oz.	5-oz.	½-pt.	1-pt.	1-qt.
7s.	12s.	18s.	24s.	36s. per gross.

WIDE-MOUTH BOTTLES,
FOR FURNITURE CREAM AND DISINFECTING POWDER.

2-oz.	3-oz.	4-oz.	5-oz.	6-oz.	8-oz.
5s.	6s. 6d.	7s. 6d.	8s.	9s.	10s. 6d.
10-oz.	12-oz.	16-oz.	24-oz.		
12s.	13s.	16s.	24s. per gross.		

FIRE BALLS kept in stock. FIRE BACKS made to order.

PACKAGES.

Crates, 3s. 6d. ; Straw & Cord, 2s. ; Cribs, 2s. ; Straw & Cord, 1s. 6d.   Hogsheads and Straw, 9s.   Tierces and Straw, 6s.
Allowance on returned packages as charged

A page from Doulton's catalogue dated 1886
(A gross is 12 dozen = 144)

Transfer Printing

Transfer printing first appeared around 1850. The process involved engraving a design onto a copper plate which was then inked and used to print a paper transfer. The transfer was applied to the pot, coated in glaze and fired in the kiln. The final product had a sharp print permanently protected by the glaze. Transfer printing was first used on potlids, but it was not long before it was being applied to many other pots and jars.

With the arrival of this printing process it became possible to supply a wide variety of household products in individual stoneware containers carrying highly detailed information about the product and supplier clearly printed on the surface. Initially this type of print was quite expensive, but as the technique improved, more potteries adopted its use and prices fell. By the early 1900s transfer printed containers had largely replaced the impressed variety and a new era of packaging had arrived. Soon many daily products such as cream, ginger beer, meat paste, marmalade, stout, medicine, ointment, polish, health food and ammonia was being sold in printer jars. Transfer printing was even used on more unusual items like foot warmers and sanitary ware.

As well as giving details of the product and manufacturer, many pots had detailed trademarks or logos to persuade potential customers that their product was better than a competitor's. Occasionally a firm would use a picture of their factory as a trademark, but these are quite rare, as are items printed in more than one colour.

A small number of companies supplying products to the Royal family were granted Royal warrants and allowed to show the monarch's coat of arms and the words "By appointment to...(whoever)". This was a useful selling point and it was not uncommon for other companies to print a fictitious coat of arms to imply royal patronage. Several firms used either the name, or even a picture of a member of the Royal family to help sell their products, judging from the many varieties supposedly used by Queen Victoria and Princess Alexandra, both must have spent a great deal of time eating anchovy pastes and brushing their teeth.

A huge variety of printing styles and type faces were available and many items carry three or four different typestyles, these range from simple block capitals to ornate scrollwork and flowing script. As with those who engraved plates used to emboss bottles many of the craftsmen involved in transfer printing were highly skilled but completely illiterate and treated letters as shapes to be copied. Unsurprisingly, occasional spelling mistakes are found. One of the best known is a variety of Burgess potlid in which the Savoy Steps in the address is spelt Savey. I have also seen a number of ginger beers with an S printed backwards.

Some companies only used one size of transfer no matter what size the container. The print can appear insignificant on a large pot but looks as if it was a job to squeeze it all on to a smaller size. (Virol food pots can sometimes be like this.)

As with glass bottles, the range of transfer printed items is so large that it is necessary to break it down into groups such as cream pots, ginger beers or potlids and deal with each separately. Whatever the category, many of the containers are highly decorative and look just right in a kitchen. By far the most popular type of jar is the one for Keiller's Dundee Marmalade which is useful for holding kitchen tools, drinking straws or pencils. A few of our guests have been surprised to find their milk served from a Victorian cream pot or mustard from a jar advertising Sainsbury meat paste.

Potlids

Potlids come in a range of sizes from about one to four inches in diameter. The miniature sizes are rare and eagerly sought, especially those bearing the words Free Sample. Most lids are circular, square or rectangular, round ones being most common, a small number of oval lids are also known and I have seen one triangular shape.

There are two distinct categories, multicoloured and monochrome. At one time the latter were seen to be the most desirable and their value has risen slowly and steadily, however, during the last decade a surge of interest in monochrome lids has seen their value rising at a much faster rate.

Multicoloured

The process for printing in several colours was developed by Felix Pratt of Fenton in Staffordshire and this type of printed lid is often referred to as Prattware despite it being produced by other potteries such as the Cauldon Pottery and Mayer's of Burslem. Much of Pratt's design work and engraving was carried out by Jesse Austin, a talented artist who spent over 30 years working for the company. Although many lids bear original Pratt designs, some carry copies of pictures by artists such as Landseer. Pratt ceased production in 1880 due mainly to the high costs involved.

These brightly coloured lids were once used to attract customers into buying pastes made from the shrimps caught in Pegwell Bay on the Sussex coast, bears grease, or the meat and fish pastes produced by firms such as Crosse and Blackwell. Just occasionally coloured lids are recovered from Victorian rubbish dumps but they are quite unusual, in 20 years of digging I have found less than 30.

Pratt's designs were not just confined to potlids but were also used on plates, bowls and vases which has led to world wide interest in the subject and has put the category of coloured potlids into the realms of the antique collector rather than that of bottle collecting. The auctioneers, Phillips, hold regular sales in London and a number of dealers specialise solely in Prattware.

Some lids have been copied over the years (I have dug four from a 1920s tip) and even in the early 1960s Elsenham reproduced a few (but they cannot be passed off as originals since the fact that they are reproductions is printed on the back). Early copies are referred to in the antiques world as "Late Issues".

Monochrome

This term simply means that any decoration or printing in a single colour, usually black on a white background, but blue, green and red prints are found, as are coloured backgrounds.

During the latter half of the nineteenth century many toothpastes, shaving creams, ointments and cold creams were sold in stoneware pots whose lids carried transfer printed details of the contents and the supplier. The first potlids appeared around 1840, hand made with flat tops and printed in blue, this being the only colour that could be produced at that time. By 1860 printing techniques had improved and it was possible to provide black print. Lids were now being pressed out and usually had domed tops.

Between 1880 and 1900 the cost of production had fallen to a level where small chemists and village stores could afford personalised pots and many took advantage of this. In his book *The Price Guide To Black And White Potlids*, Ronald Dale catalogues about 2,500 lids and this is by no means a full listing. New lids are found quite regularly with local interest often being strong enough to put a £30 - £50 price tag on even the most mundane examples.

For some time there has been a shortage of potlids and this has forced up prices for common lids from the £5-10 price range of a few years ago to around three times that. At the other end of the market top quality pictorial lids have always proved to be a good investment and there appears to be no shortage of potential buyers willing to pay out hundreds of pounds for prized specimens.

The earliest pots held bears' grease. As its name suggests, this was the fat from the carcass of a dead bear mixed with perfume for men to use on their hair as an early form of Brylcream. Part of its appeal was that it was thought to help promote growth of the hair since few bald bears are ever seen. However, despite advertising which claimed that the grease was genuine and originated from Russian bears, some were no more than perfumed goose or mutton fat.

Bears' greases are the rarest category of potlids, the product could cost anything up to a guinea and only the rich could afford to spend this sort of sum, consequently there are relatively few around. Whilst no bears' grease potlid can be considered common, the most frequently found is one for James Atkinson of 24 Bond Street, London, in the 2/6d size and the price of one of these today is around £30. This lid has a trademark of a chained bear and stems from Atkinson's early days when he used a live bear outside his premises for advertising.

The majority of potlids contained toothpaste. This was not the same texture we know today, but came as a solid block of paste, sometimes ground cuttlefish bones being used as an ingredient to ensure a coarse consistency. It was often flavoured with Areca (Betel) nut which was also used as a medicine to get rid of worms, a common complaint with the poor quality food in Victorian days. Few consumers were aware that by cleaning the teeth they were ensuring that they were unlikely to suffer from worms. Some Areca nut lids can be found with a picture of palm trees and a mosque, or sometimes simply a picture of the nut itself.

Cherry toothpaste was almost as popular as areca nut, this is not too surprising since it was exactly the same preparation, but with carmine added which gave it a red coloration. Despite having never been anywhere near a cherry, lids were produced showing a bunch of them as a trademark. Other toothpastes contained ingredients such as Honeysuckle or charcoal and some used carbolic (which must have tasted dreadful). Some were advertised as being saponaceous, which meant that they foamed in the mouth.

Cold cream and, less frequently, shaving cream and pomade for the hair was also supplied in these pots, often being scented with almond oil. Another perfume used was otto of rose that naturally led to some suppliers using a picture of roses on their lids as a trademark. Pots were also produced which only bore the words Cold Cream. These appear in a number of variations and were a stock item bought by chemists who filled the pots with their own preparations and stuck a paper label on the pot showing details of contents and the supplier.

Another popular line for potlids was fish pastes and potted meats. Anchovy paste, bloater paste and potted tongue were quite common, but how these were kept fresh before refrigerators is anybody's guess, it is likely that gastric disorders were common amongst consumers. Easily the most popular anchovy paste was produced by James Burgess, his use of the Royal Coat of Arms as a trademark makes dating them simple as the coat of arms changed with the monarch. Additionally, in 1902 they moved from 107 The Strand to Hythe Road, Willesden, therefore the early address is Victorian and the later address is not. (The company still trades in specialist sauces and prepared foods.)

Other recognised names using these pots were Crosse and Blackwell and Fortnum and Mason, both having a coat of arms printed on the lid. The most attractive group of potlids are those used by Blanchflower of Great Yarmouth (Norfolk). They are large sized pictorial lids, one of which shows a fishing boat, another has a picture of a barrel of anchovies and one shows a group of farmyard animals.

Some of the quack cure brigade also used this type of packaging for their cure-alls, probably the best known being the Holloways Ointment lids which come in several sizes. Mannina Herbal Ointment was a series of lids where each type was numbered with a list of ailments that it was supposed to cure. No.1 was for the treatment of cancer and tumours, No.2 for sore legs and ulcerated wounds, No.3 apparently cured eczema, scurvy and psoriasis (amongst others). The most dangerous substance was that contained in the pots whose lids bear the name of Doctor Shower. This was supposed to cure cancerous growths and was actually radium salve, there is no record of its effect on its users, nor on the workers who prepared and packed it.

Other cures included hair restorers. I have an advertisement which advises users to wear gloves when applying the ointment to prevent the growth of unsightly hair on the hands and fingers. Lip salves and eye ointments occasionally turn up, as do such oddities as a pot that once held moustache wax.

Cream Pots

Most of today's cream is bought from shops with a small quantity being delivered to our doorsteps by the milkman. In the 19th century the situation was rather different when the majority of milk and cream was delivered by horse drawn cart from a local dairy or farm. The lady of the house had milk measured directly into her jug from a churn on the cart (no milk bottles in those days) and cream was supplied in little pots. The problem of keeping milk fresh before refrigeration was overcome by the milk roundsman covering the route two or three times a day. Customers bought just sufficient for their immediate needs (late morning deliveries were often called the milk pudding round).

Life could be hard for milkmen, working days of over 14 hours being commonplace, horses were groomed between rounds and the harness, carts and dairy equipment cleaned and polished. In Richmond (Surrey) where I grew up, horses from one local dairy were required to pull the horse drawn fire engine in an emergency. Despite long hours and hard work, research into defunct local dairies shows that many employees stayed with the same company throughout their working lives.

By the 1870s dairies were selling cream in simple stoneware pots with either a chocolate brown or a saltglazed finish. There were two common types, both some 3 inches tall and the same basic shape, one was a simple round pot (called an ali-baba) and the other had a handle and pouring lip. Both types were sealed with a muslin or waxed paper lid secured with string and, when empty, were just thrown away in the same way that we dump our plastic yoghurt cartons today. These cheap mass produced pots were extremely popular and still used in some places as late as the mid 1920s.

Transfer printing enabled shops, dairies and farms to supply cream in personalised containers showing details of both the product and supplier. Some had pictorial trademarks in the form of a rustic scene such as the farm, a milkmaid or a cow. Road travel was a slow process before the motor car but a reliable and efficient railway system meant that cream could be made in Devon one day and on sale right across the country the next. One Devonshire company used a small railway engine and the words "Per Rail Daily" on their pots.

A standard printed cream pot has black print on a white or cream background, the shoulder and lip often being given a brown glaze (two tone). Green and blue topped varieties occasionally turn up and, more rarely, pots printed in some colour other than black. The straight sided cylinders that once held clotted cream are a more unusual shape but a large proportion of them have coloured printing, these are known in green, blue, red, purple and sepia.

Britain's largest supplier of dairy equipment was The Dairy Supply Company but most potteries were happy to supply pots printed to order, (one London dairy had their cream pots made by Coalport). The standard of printing was usually very high, probably the best being those from Port Dundas in Glasgow who made the well known Wigtownshire Creamery pots with a picture of a milkmaid with a three legged stool and a milk pail. Irish cream pots were often made by the Belleck pottery.

Even fairly common cream pots can be attractive. The combination of different shapes, sizes, colours and pictorial trademarks have helped make them a major collecting line. During the late 1980s cream pots suddenly took off amongst collectors and values rocketed, items were being sold with over £300 price tags. Although much of the frenzy has now gone out of the market, top quality items are still appreciating well above the rate of inflation, one fetching £1,900 at auction.

Although a bank loan may be needed to buy just a few of the ultra rare items, there are plenty of nice pots to be found at much more sensible prices, e.g. the two toned Hailwoods pots (in three sizes) and the off-white Manchester Creamery both have cows as trademarks and can be picked up for under £5. Cylinders turn up rather less often and this is reflected in their prices. In 1989 to 1990 quantities of Horner's pots turned up on a dump in Wales, prior to this they carried a £20-30 price tag, but when large numbers came on the market the value dropped by half. Today they are back to their original price. This cylinder is printed in red and carries an advert for cream cheese on the front, it also has a dozen or so lines of blurb on the back extolling its virtues and claiming recommendation from the medical fraternity. Today doctors warn of the high cholesterol levels in cream.

Printed pots are not only extremely attractive, but they look just right on a shelf in any kitchen and the simple brown and saltglazed creams are ideal for a display of small dried plants.

Caviar Pots

Caviare (old spelling) has always been a luxury product, but there was far more consumed 75 to 100 years ago than there is today. The pots which once held the product were very strong with thick walls to help keep the caviar cold when it was taken out of storage and this is the reason why so many have survived to be recovered from old rubbish tips. A one ounce serving of caviar may well have been sold in a pot which weighed half a pound.

The standard shape is a squat stoneware cylinder with three large slots cut into the top. They were sealed with a flat stoneware disc which had a three pronged metal clasp fitted, the prongs of the clasp fitted into the slots and turned to lock the lid into place.

A "fun" caviar display by the author for the Surrey bottle show

Most are finished in an off-white glaze, sometimes having a honey coloured top, and transfer printed. Earlier containers are usually saltglazed and these can also be found in bulbous shape looking rather like a barrel with incised lettering. There are also a number of two tone and white glazed pots with several lines of incised writing with the supplier's name and address and details of the product. The rarest caviar pots are cylindrical and I only know of two suppliers who used these, Monoroff and W.G. White.

The most commonly found pots are those from Fortnum and Mason who used both the standard shape (in both white and two toned finish) and a range of different sized potlids whose bases carried a picture of a sturgeon. All their containers are decorated with a Royal Warrant and it is possible to build up a collection of well over 30 pots spanning more than a century from just this single company. Today they sell a pot whose lid carries an Elizabeth II coat of arms and a postcode as part of the company address.

Other major London department stores that used printed pots include William Whiteley, Jackson of Piccadilly, Harrods and Selfridges. It was even possible for gentlemen to buy pots of caviar from their "club". I have examples from Buck's, Master's and Nash's clubs.

There were a large number of small companies using these pots, some added a royal coat of arms, a two headed eagle and the Prince of Wales feathers to indicate some sort of royal connection. This was usually a marketing ploy for a product aimed at the richer

members of a society where social standing played a huge part. Other firms used a Russian connection in their names to show that they supplied genuine caviar, these include the Russian Tea Rooms, the Astrachan Caviare Co, and the Russian and Oriental Produce Co.

I have been collecting these pots for a number of years and when I started there was a large choice. It was possible to buy common examples for £8-£10, today the price is more often around £25. Although they are not quite as thick on the ground, there are still plenty to be found. Before I became more sensible about collecting them I had pots from over 50 different companies plus double that in different sizes and variations.

Ginger Beer

Ginger beer became extremely popular in the late Victorian era and by the turn of the century outsold every other type of drink except beer. Although classed as a soft drink, it was actually alcoholic.

The recipe was quite simple - mix bruised ginger, sugar, lemon and cream of tartar in boiling water. Allow to cool, add yeast and allow to ferment, then strain and bottle.

One problem was that secondary fermentation was common, some firms actually fermented it in the bottle and the pressure generated in this process could cause glass bottles to explode. For this reason ginger beer was supplied in stoneware bottles which were strong enough to contain the pressure and prevented customers from seeing the unsightly residue in the bottom of the bottle. Between 1880 & 1900 thick walled black glass bottles were tried, but these were expensive and proved unreliable. Stoneware bottles was so successful that the terms Stone Brewed or Stone Ginger Beer became commonly used.

The earliest ginger beer bottles were slip glazed, but these were soon replaced with saltglazed versions which were in general use until the early 1900s.

Bottles usually have the brewers name incised into the body or shoulder. Customers only bought the drink, the bottle remained the property of the supplier and some firms charged a refundable deposit on the bottle so that it would be returned for re-use. There was a dislike of this practice amongst customers and a few companies added the words "No Deposit Charged" as a sales pitch. This explains why large numbers of ginger beer bottles can be found in Victorian rubbish dumps.

During the early part of the 20th century transfer printing started to replace saltglazing. A few firms saved on cost by having their saltglazed bottles overprinted, but soon the standard ginger beer bottle was either all white or white bodied with a honey coloured top and details of the supplier printed under the glaze. A champagne shaped variety of saltglazed bottle was brought back for a short period around 1910 by two of the largest suppliers, R. White and Batey, to hold their "old fashioned" ginger beers.

With such a simple brewing process, little back street operations existed and it was not unusual for them to save on the cost of buying bottles and simply use any they could get their hands on. To stop this pirating some companies used bottles with distinctive coloured tops which could be instantly identified, even if still in a crate.

Other companies went one stage further and used both coloured tops and coloured printing, but this was more to catch the customer's eye rather than for any security purposes. The most common colours are green and blue, red and pink are more unusual. Coloured top ginger beers are often rare and command relatively high prices.

As competition increased some suppliers tried to attract customers by using pictorial trademarks. Some of these are superb examples of transfer printing and carry highly detailed pictures of buildings, people, animals and transport, two showing fully rigged sailing ships. Unfortunately there is quite a demand for the better pictorials and some can change hands for hundreds of pounds.

Early ginger beers were sealed with cork hammered into place and wired in for added security. The blob top was designed to give the top of the bottle the extra strength needed to withstand this treatment. Sometimes bottles have a small hole drilled through the blob, this is a "Galtee More" patent which used a metal pin to hold the cork in place. The cork was usually replaced by the internal screw thread, but a number of firms moved to the swing stopper. This was more popular in Scotland than England.

Towards the end of the 1920s changes were taking place and ginger beer was fully brewed before bottling. This meant that glass bottles, usually in brown or green, could be used and suppliers also changed to the cheaper crown cap. A few firms continued to use stone bottles well into the 1930s. Often these being an unusually large size, these were normally advertised as containing "old fashioned" or "original" ginger beer, strange to think that nostalgia was being used as a marketing ploy seventy years ago.

Another collecting line is miniature ginger beers, some were made as promotional pieces or travellers samples, others were for use in dolls houses. The saltglazed Doulton pieces are most often seen and these range in size from around a quarter to two inches in height. Much rarer are transfer printed examples and at the top of the range are coloured top varieties which can fetch several hundred pounds.

Unfortunately real brewed ginger beer is no longer made although some soft drink makers are trying to kid us that their cans contain the real thing - look at the label, E - additives did not exist a century ago. At one time a glass of shandy was a mixture of bitter (ale) and ginger beer, today a mix of chemically brewed beer and citric acid flavoured lemonade is served up as an insipid copy.

Ointment Pots

Ointment pots have a long history and archaeologists have found them on Roman sites. Between 1600 and the mid 1800s they were commonly used by apothecaries. These early pots (called albarellos) were often Dutch made with a tin glaze finish and sometimes decorated with a crosshatch design in blue, they were generally larger than those from Victoria's reign. Another type occasionally found is shaped like an oversized egg cup, these sometimes carry the chemist's name. However, both types are extremely rare and collectors tend to concentrate on the transfer printed variety which became more widely available in the latter part of the 18th century. Despite only being a couple of inches tall, many carry up to a dozen lines of printing giving a list of ailments the ointment would supposedly treat.

Most of these pots were used by the type of confidence trickster that produced quack cures and owed their considerable success more to the advertising copy writer than any medical grounds. Many ointments were advertised as being universal cure-alls, suitable for the treatment of almost any known ailment. Samuel Moorcroft's Good Samaritan Ointment supposedly cured a huge range of ailments including bad eyes and piles.

The usual price for a small pot of ointment was one shilling, the purchaser also had to pay for the tax levied on medicines at that time. Having a tax stamp printed on a label gave the impression that there was some form of government approval of the contents. To distance themselves from any implied responsibility, the stamp later carried the wording "This stamp bears no guarantee".

The best known and widest advertised ointment was Holloway's. There are five different versions of the pot as well as several potlids for this preparation which claims to cure sore legs, gout, rheumatism and bad breasts. Most of his pots carry a picture of a seated lady who represents Purity, but in fact a large proportion of the contents was no more than beeswax. Holloway sold his ointment and pills world wide and spent vast amounts of money on advertising. His most audacious act was to bribe Egyptian authorities to allow him to advertise his concoction on the pyramids. Holloway was an out and out charlatan who made a fortune from his worthless medicines, but he put some of his money to good use by building the Holloway Sanatorium and the Holloway College which was visited by Queen Victoria. The building still stands at the top of Egham hill in Surrey where it is still used as a college.

The second most widely found pot is Clarke's Miraculous Salve which is found in two sizes. Later versions are in a semi transparent china and great care must be taken when cleaning as the print is sometimes over the glaze and can be lost in chemical cleaning or if rubbed too hard. Clarke's (of Lincoln) also made a quack cure called the "World Famed Blood Mixture".

Another well-known pot carries no claims at all and is printed in blue. Although its trade name was Poor Man's Friend, it was actually no cheaper than most of the others. This was made by Beach and Barnicote who managed to get some sort of medical connection by claiming to be "Successors to Dr. Roberts of Bridport".

Also claiming medical attachment is the very rare "Dr Rookes Golden Ointment" with a trademark of a phoenix rising from the ashes. It also claims to have been Discovered A.D. 1839 and was rather expensive at two shillings and ninepence per pot.

Another sought after pot called the No Name Ointment was produced by a Mr. Whitehouse from Birmingham. It carries a clever trademark of a white house. Unfortunately this pot has been faked and, until suspicion was raised by large numbers appearing on the scene, some respected dealers and collectors were taken in. No doubt some of these fakes will remain in circulation for a while.

There are two sizes of Natures Herbal Ointment to be found. The pots are of a long cylindrical shape without the normal high glaze finish, printing is often of a poor standard and written lengthways rather than across the pot. This one advertises itself as being able to cure a huge variety of complaints including spinal diseases and epilepsy.

The Singleton's Eye and Golden Eye Ointments are an unusual shape, being almost flat. All the buyer received was a thin smear which was just enough to fill a shallow depression in the top. This was covered with a paper disc and occasionally these turn up in their original card boxes.

But not all ointments were fraudulent preparations. Included in the category are an extract of sarsaparilla produced by Boots, a carbolic ointment from the Parkes Drug Company and a number of Lanolin lotions, some of which have unusual red, green or orange prints. The range can also be extended by including a number of potlids which were once used for ointments.

Most ointments disappeared from the market soon after the turn of the century when they were analysed by the medical authorities both here and in America who published listings of their contents in an attempt to stem the flow of quack medicines.

Ointments are comparatively expensive with prices starting around £10 and running up into several hundred pounds. However, despite their comparatively high prices, they can make a delightful collecting line since they take up little space, yet have interesting printing which covers a wide range of different typestyles.

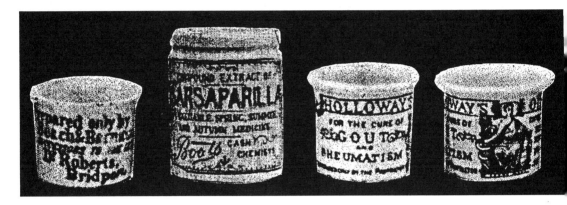

Clay Pipes

Tobacco was first introduced into Britain during the mid 1560s and was smoked not only for its novelty value, but also for its supposedly medicinal properties. The plant was first imported into Europe from America around 1561 by Jean Nicot, a Frenchman from whose name the word Nicotine is derived.

The earliest pipes were copies of the ceremonial pipes used by the American Indians and had tiny bowls. This doubtless helped to reduce smoking costs since tobacco was prohibitively expensive (in 1600 its price was about £2.50 a pound). At that time there was no suitable material available for making pipes and many made from gold or silver and decorated with precious stones. It must have been quite painful to smoke them.

It was another 30 years before Kaolin (or Pipe Clay) was found in Dorset and the first clay pipes were made. These were not treated as anything other than an extra line for established potteries, but soon demand led to specialist potteries being set up to cater to the new fashion. In a very short time English clay pipes were being exported all around the world.

Competition started to flourish as other European countries found deposits of pipe clay and established their own potteries. The Dutch, who had no pipe clay of their own, imported their Kaolin from England and then exported clay pipes back to Britain at prices that were cheap enough to threaten the home industry. Protection was given to British producers in 1663 when Parliament banned the export of pipe clay.

During the reign of Elizabeth I tobacco was taxed at 2d (less than one new penny) a pound. When James I came to the throne he increased the tax by over forty times to nearly 7 shillings.

Trials in home growing were already taking place and the huge price increase set off further experimentation, but the idea was to prove short lived with the home growing of tobacco being made illegal. Those who attempted to ignore the ban found their crop destroyed by a troop of cavalry riding over their fields and faced a large fine. James, like succeeding monarchs and Chancellors of the Exchequer, realised the value of the weed to the country's coffers.

Early clay pipes had thick stems and were about 10 cms long. The small bowl was set at an angle of about 45 degrees and the bottom of the bowl (heel) was flattened so that the pipe could be stood upright when not in use. Later this was changed to a small spur protruding from the base of the bowl. Over the years, as the relative price of tobacco came down, the shape gradually altered and bowls became larger and more upright. Stems became thinner and slowly increased in length to around 45 cms by the mid 1700s, gradually reducing again to about 20 cms by the end of the 19th century.

Around 1800 it became fashionable to use a type of pipe known as a "Churchwarden" which had a stem about a meter in length. At the other extreme, Victorian navvies often used a pipe with a stem only 3 or 4 cms long known as a noseburner. This was not quite the silly design it seems since it could be used in the rain, the bowl being protected by the wide brimmed hats which they wore.

The change in shape was a slow evolutionary process and took around 300 years. This means that pipes can be dated fairly accurately simply from their size and shape. If the bowl is set at right angles to the stem or carries some decoration, it is almost certain that the pipe is Victorian.

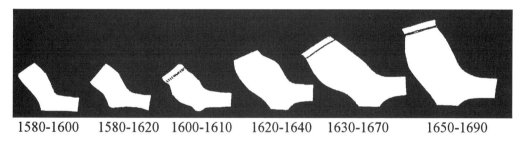

1580-1600   1580-1620   1600-1610   1620-1640   1630-1670   1650-1690

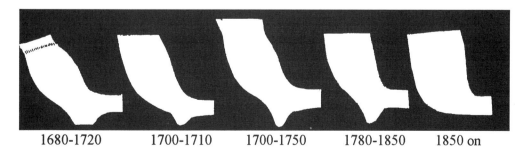

1680-1720   1700-1710   1700-1750   1780-1850   1850 on

Some producers marked their pipes with either their initials or, more rarely, a pottery mark, early marks are generally impressed into the pipe and later ones embossed. If initials are found on one side of the heel of a pipe then the right hand letter indicates the surname. If initials are marked on either side of the spur then, when the pipe is held in the smoking position, the letter on the left is that of the Christian name and that on the right the surname. It is not unusual to find Victorian examples showing the full makers' name and/or the name of the pipe style running down the stem.

Early pipes are normally quite plain, the only decoration being the occasional milled line around the top. The increase in competition brought about by a tremendous growth in the tobacco industry during the Victorian era (London alone had over 100 pipe manufacturers in 1880) forced makers into new ideas to try and catch the customer's eye. The decorating of pipe bowls became popular and soon smokers were able to purchase pipes which carried a relief moulding of almost any subject: e.g. animals, transport, sports, military crests, buildings, famous people, special events.

Pipes were also produced in the form of miniature busts. Royalty, politicians, military leaders and entertainers were common subjects. Others were made in the shape of animals such as horses, fish, dogs birds and even elephants. Some (known as grotesques) were made to represent the devil or in the shape of skulls. There were several bawdy subjects, one example is a well proportioned lady sitting on a chamber pot (shown top left in the photo below). Some of the most collectable pipes came from the Gambier factory in France. Many came in their own lined cases and had detachable amber or ivory stems. A number of Gambier's catalogues have survived and their range of products has been well researched by pipe societies world wide.

Clay pipes were an extremely cheap product which were even used as targets on fairground rifle ranges. Some publicans had a glass filled with pipes on the bar for customers to use. Once smoked they would be put in a fire to burn off any tobacco residue and turn them white again.

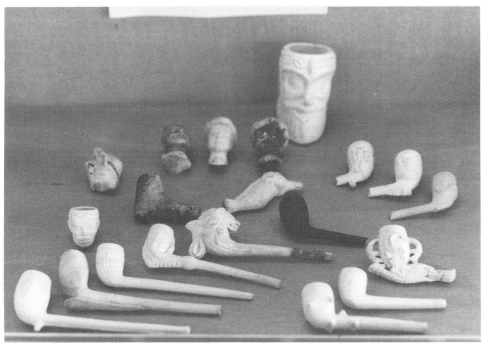

Victorian Clay Pipes. This collection includes a giant advertising pipe
and a horse's head which had a detachable stem.

The arrival of the cigarette dealt the knell blow to the clay pipe industry and, as their popularity rocketed, pipe manufacturers quickly went out of business. A few managed to hold out for a short while by selling their products to toy shops as children's bubble pipes, but it was a losing battle and during the short period between 1900 and the end of the First World War the industry had collapsed.

Today there are two manufacturers producing clay pipes as a novelty line, Nikko Pipes (Barnstaple in Devon) and Eric Ayto. Some of their pipes are made in original moulds but these are fairly easy to tell from older versions as the clay of a different texture. However both ensure that their products cannot be used to deceive by using a distinct makers mark of a circle containing either an N for Nikko or an 8 for Ayto.

Before its sad demise the Bramber Pipe Museum in Sussex had over 45,000 pipes and smoking related items in its collection so there is a huge scope in this collecting line. Good figurals can fetch £20-30. A few years ago I was shown a large highly detailed pipe in the form of the god Pan sitting on a throne which had just changed hands for £170.

A mixed stoneware display. Note the pot fourth from right top shelf universally known as a non-drip ink - this example is transfer printed *Ellis's Universal Embrocation for horses and cattle*

Part of the author's stock at his bottle stall in the Horse Hospital at
Camden's Stables Market (PL)

Part II: Digging for bottles

Chapter 5: Bottle Digging

Old bottles can be found at collectors fairs, auctions, antique shops and shows as well as the cheaper venues such as car boot sales, flea markets, charity shops and on market stalls. Usually they only appear in small numbers, often in poor condition and then only the more common items. But just occasionally a rare item will turn up. In 1994 a young student paid six pounds for a box of assorted bottles. I realised one item was particularly rare and arranged for it to go for auction for her where it sold for £1,150.

Building a collection from these sources can be a time consuming business in which it might take years just to get a few basics. If you are very lucky you may come across one of a limited number of specialist dealers who will usually have a much larger display than is normally seen. Although it is possible to collect without spending a fortune, it will still cost something and there is always that special item whose price puts it out of reach. A budget may stretch to five pounds a week to for bottles but few can afford to pay out £1,000 for a rarity.

But suppose I were to tell you that it is possible to get a collection, including some of the scarcer items, entirely free of charge - no that is not a misprint, it costs nothing at all. What is more, you will also get spares to sell on and help pay for those items which cost more than you can really afford to spend.

Collecting for nothing

Every week thousands of collectors all over the country do just that, spending their spare time digging up bottles from long forgotten rubbish dumps. Many dumps are over 100 years old and hold huge numbers of collectable bottles and pots which are only yesterday's packaging, thrown away when empty like our yoghurt cartons and beer cans today. Bottle digging is basically a matter of tracking down where rubbish was buried and digging it up again.

This hobby must be almost unique as it needs no special equipment or expensive outlay to start, it is free to participate and it is normal to show a profit at the end of the day. Regular digging exercises the muscles and keeps you fit. Some think that it seems hard work, but it is only necessary to put in as much, or as little, effort as you want. It can be great fun with the occasional burst of excitement, with over 20 years digging experience I still get a buzz when something unusual turns up.

Where to start

I am regularly asked "Where can I dig up bottles?" Unfortunately there is no easy answer to this, locating a site is not just a matter of looking for the words Rubbish Dump on an old map. It can be a time consuming business, taking a fair bit of detective work combined with more than a little walking and searching. At other times an area just seems to shout "dig here". There is nothing magical about finding an old dump as there are often clues to be found. The trick is to recognise these clues and interpret them.

Almost from the first day I started the in hobby I have been told that "all the sites have dried up and there is nowhere left to dig". This is untrue, there are still many thousands of dumps waiting to be found by anybody prepared to put in a little time and effort. As with everything in life, there is no substitute for experience - but all bottle diggers were once novices and would not be in the hobby now if they had not found their first dump. I usually get in a day or two's digging when I go on holiday and have found dumps as far apart as Devon and the Scottish Highlands.

Finding a site can be just a matter of basic observation or reasoning. For example:- Farmers tend to use every square inch of land, I found one farm dump by investigating a small stand of trees growing in the middle of a cultivated field. The reason that these trees had not been removed was that they stood on three feet of rubbish which made the patch unsuitable for farming.

Luck can also play a part: some years ago I was driving in some heavy traffic and noticed that the truck in front was carrying a load of earth sprinkled with bits of aqua glass and china. I followed it to where the load was dumped (this was out of bounds) and back to where it had picked up its load. I ended up with permission to dig a Victorian dump which was being removed before redevelopment.

Finding your own dump

The starting point in finding a site is to think about the most likely areas to search. It is preferable to pick somewhere fairly close to home so that it is possible to nip out for an hour or two to check possibilities. It is also worth considering what is likely to have been thrown away, rubbish from a small village is unlikely to hold as many quality items as that from a country house. Working men could not afford two shillings for a jar of ointment to put on a burn or a shilling for a pot of toothpaste. They would have put goose fat on a scald and cleaned their teeth with salt.

Usually better quality items will be found in rubbish dumps associated with the richer members of society. High on the list would be spa towns such as Cheltenham, Harrogate or Bath plus the Victorian holiday resorts. But don't fret if there are none of these nearby. I live near Heathrow Airport, about 50 miles from the nearest beach and even further from the closest watering place, yet I have had my share of treasures.

If you are a city dweller or live in a large town, then its dump(s) were likely to have been sited on the outskirts, just those areas where a lot of redevelopment work has taken place in recent years, many old dumps are now covered by superstores, car parks, industrial units and office blocks. Since bottle digging has been going for decades then it is quite possible that your town's municipal dumps have already been found and dug out and it may be better to concentrate on areas outside the larger towns.

Maps

The first requirement for hunting dumps is a large scale Ordinance Survey map of the area, this is used as a master document for recording and pinpointing possible areas for searching. The next step is to visit to your town's main library which should hold large scale maps of the area going back 100 years or more and updated versions which appeared every 10 or 20 years. There is normally only a small fee for a copy and it is worth getting photocopies of the complete range from 1850 to around 1930 for the area that you are interested in. These maps are an invaluable source of reference (even if they do not say "Rubbish Dump"). With just one old map it is possible to immediately identify a likely rubbish dump. Just look for a sewerage, gas or brick works which should go right at the top of the list of places to check (see section on types of dump).

Carefully compare features on one map with those on another (say) 20 years later. Look out for lakes, ponds, canals, quarries, pits or areas of marshland which are no longer shown, and where new embankments have been built. Each is a starting point for your investigations. Once likely areas have been noted, transfer their locations onto your current edition Ordinance Survey map to pinpoint the exact place to search.

Research

Invaluable information on the location of rubbish tips can be found in old records. A couple of days spent on research is more likely to yield the location of an old rubbish tip than a month of wandering around the countryside on the off-chance.

The first port of call is the municipal library in which you should find sufficient material to keep you going for months. Do not expect to find any reference books on dumps or rubbish - I have yet to find one. Instead you are looking for background information and clues to help you decide where to start searching. Tell the librarian what you are looking for and there is a good chance that a member of staff will have enough local history knowledge to be able point out the best place to look for information. Read up every bit of local history including old diaries in the reference section.

Another point of enquiry is the municipal offices. Council archives may record the minutes of meetings in which the subject of refuse disposal was discussed. They could also record complaints from residents regarding unpleasant smells and insects or about fly tipping (illegal dumping). Some archives hold Borough Surveyors' reports which can be an invaluable source of information.

Many towns have a local newspaper which has been going since the last century and it is usually possible to use back copies for research. If this is the case in your area then take full advantage as these papers are likely to carry reports and readers' letters covering actual or proposed sites. Sometimes the matter was discussed for weeks and it is possible that articles or complaints about fly tipping will also appear. One Surrey dump turned up when a club member found a 1909 report covering heated arguments between adjoining councils with one accusing the other of dumping its refuse on its land.

Publicity

Sometimes information on possible sites comes from the most unexpected sources. If you let it be known that your free time is spent seeking out where rubbish was buried 100 years ago, then digging it up again, you may find that some of your neighbours will cross the road when they see you coming and treat the rest of your family with sympathy. But, just occasionally, it will yield results when you are told that "there are loads of old bottles at ...."

Free newspapers are always looking for local news to help pad out the advertisements and local papers love to report on the strange hobbies of their readers. You are likely to get some free publicity if you contact them, but be prepared for it to be treated as a bit of a joke. It is advisable to suggest that you are unearthing social history rather than treasure hunting. Never discuss values or the headline could be "Local man digs up fortune" and you will need to increase your insurance policies and security.

Other sources

The local museum is certainly worth a visit. Have a chat with the curator, even if he has no knowledge on the subject he might know someone who has.

Why not join the local history society, perhaps somebody may have found the information you are seeking while researching some other subject.

Pay an occasional visit to your local council offices and check planning applications. Most are for small jobs such as house extensions or changes of purpose, but major building scheme will also be on record. It would be a shame to go past a spot which you suspected of being a dump only to find a new superstore sitting on it.

I have been told about possible sites by metal detector users who had no interest in bottle digging, it may be worth checking whether there is a club in your area. Again, this information should be in the library.

Cultivate local builders, gas and electricity workers, cable TV installers and (especially) JCB drivers, many have come across dumps whilst working on building sites. It is worth the outlay of a few pints of falling over water to find a Victorian dump. I have even had digger drivers open up a hole for the price of a couple of drinks.

Other people worth talking to are those who spend a great deal of their time out in the country, such as walkers, bird watchers, rough shooters and fishermen. Even better are the somewhat shady characters such as scrap metal collectors, totters and those who use ferrets for rabbit hunting (or even poachers if you know of any). Who is more likely to come across a dump than someone who spends his time in out of the way places?

Rubbish disposal

Between 1750 and 1850 there was a movement from the countryside to towns and cities where there was ample employment in manufacturing and domestic service. Some four million people were classed as town dwellers in 1751, a century later with the population doubled, around fifteen million lived in towns and cities. Each extra mouth required feeding and the quantity of prepacked goods grew year by year. This packaging, plus the debris of day to day living, was just dumped anywhere and the amount of rotting debris in the streets started to cause concern. It was not only unsightly and smelt, but lead to an alarming rise in the population of rats and insects.

The more influential members of society demanded that something be done about the situation and a number of borough councils arranged for its collection and disposal. It was only a small step to have refuse collected from houses located in the better districts. The City of London had a regular free collection service by 1830, but this was likely to have been available only to the privileged few. The refuse was taken to the City's depot at Lett's Wharf on the bank of the Thames near Blackfriars Bridge where it was sorted.

As the century progressed household collection services became more widespread, although mainly confined to the more affluent areas of the town. (This was not just a matter of looking after the richer members of society, but because the poor were very poor indeed with little to throw away).

Scavenging

Today, in order to reduce the amount of waste councils have to dispose of, tied in with saving raw materials, we are urged to recycle waste. There are collection points for paper, cardboard, plastic, bottles and empty aluminium cans. Some councils set targets for recycling and make political points from their initiatives (or is it confidence trick to save on disposal costs. I have yet to hear a reasonable explanation as to why recycled products are more expensive than those made from new).

It will probably come as a surprise to discover that at one time almost everything thrown away was recycled which not only paid for the collection service but often made a substantial profit. By the mid 1800s a number of scavenging companies had been set up. Some were private enterprises who paid a licence fee giving them collecting rights for a certain area, others were run by the councils themselves.

Rubbish was collected and taken to a transfer station or shoot where it was searched (scavenged) for anything that could be re-used. Scavengers came from amongst the poorest members of society, Often women and children who, armed with a rake and a sack waded through the heaps of refuse picking up anything that could be recycled . Their wages were about a shilling (5 new pence) a day.

Bottles went back to the brewers, mineral water suppliers and wine merchants; fruit, jam and pickle jars to bottling works; broken glass was sold to glassworks to be melted down to make new bottles (this material was called cullet); rags were sorted for re-use or cleaning; scrap metal was sold to iron foundries, biscuit and food tins often went to luggage manufacturers who used them as clamps to reinforce corners; broken china could be utilised as hard-core in road building; glue factories would buy discarded bones from the Sunday joint and even the odd animal carcass was useful to tallow makers for producing candles.

Before electricity and gas industries arrived coal was the only fuel generally available for heating and cooking and the greatest proportion of the rubbish consisted of coal ash. This was a valuable commodity much in demand by brickworks who mixed it with the clay to make bricks.

Some bottle diggers dream of having an early Victorian rubbish dump to dig, but the reality is that many of these tips hold little more than pieces of broken china and sifted ash, with just the occasional bottle. Some years ago three friends and I dug reclaimed land that once carried a railway line into London's Docklands. Trains first ran on the line in 1862. On our first trip I was lucky enough to dig up an extremely rare potlid, The Arctic Expedition, and one of my friends had another rare bears' grease lid. Naturally we got rather excited about the site's potential and could hardly wait for our next trip, but between us we clocked up 19 days digging before the next decent item came out. This rubbish had been well and truly scavenged.

During the 1870s scavenging became less viable and had largely died out by 1900. The main cause was a slump in the building trade resulting in fewer bricks being needed so that the makers were unwilling to buy the coal ash. Some brickworks accepted bulk unsorted rubbish free of charge with the intention of sifting out the ash when business picked up again. Many Kent and London based bottle diggers will fondly remember visiting one Kent brickworks which was still sifting Victorian ash in the late 1970s.

The increase in packaging was overwhelming the collection points. To reduce costs the scavengers' wages were cut (often by half) and much of the rubbish was taken directly to the dump, saving the cost of double handling at the transfer station. By this time householders had become used to having their rubbish collected and, as the scavenging companies folded, responsibility for its collection was transferred to local councils via the 1875 Public Health Act. Since then municipal authorities have had an ever growing problem of disposing of steadily increasing amounts of rubbish.

Some councils tried to reduce the volume by incinerating it prior to dumping, but the idea was not always successful and fires were commonplace. One incinerator at Blackburn (Lancashire) opened in a blaze of publicity and civic pride. Unfortunately it closed in another sort of blaze when it burnt down on its first day of operation.

Another idea for reducing the volume was to use a huge dust extractor to separate solids from the coal ash. Again these had problems, Edinburgh had one which suffered from occasional blockages in its chimney which resulted in nearby houses having their roofs covered in waste paper.

One unusual idea was patented in 1906, under the trade name Pyrojim. It involved abstracting the dust, mixing with water and compressing into blocks which could be used as fuel. The cost was estimated at 6 shillings (30p) a ton with a selling price of 12-15 shillings a ton. Pyrojim was not a commercial success, surprising when the chance of making a profit is weighed against cost of transporting rubbish - in the same year Guildford Corporation was paying a contractor 56 shillings a barge load (plus another two pounds a day for unloading).

Few authorities used these ideas and most were stuck with the problem of dumping huge quantities of refuse. Fortunately for us bottle diggers some methods of disposal were commonly used and it is possible to use this knowledge to help locate a site today, even though it may now be covered in trees and undergrowth and looks like any other piece of land.

A century ago there was less pressure on land than today, its price was fairly low and it was easy to for councils to purchase an area for a dump. Some of the dumping grounds were chosen so that refuse could be used for other purposes, such as filling in areas of marshland which would then be capped with topsoil or clay and sold for farming.

The simplest way to dispose of unwanted rubbish was to tip it into a convenient hole in the ground. As the number of suitable holes was limited other methods of disposal had to be found, consequently there are many different types of "rubbish dump". One thing to bear in mind is that when a council found a convenient way to dispose of its refuse it tried to stick to the same system. Therefore one dump can give a clue to other possible sites in that area.

Rubbish disposal sites

Sewage and gas works

A major problem with rubbish is the huge quantity to be disposed of, not only does it require large areas of land for its disposal (either above or under), but it also needs good access. Another problem is the smell and its attraction to insects and vermin, both of which are likely to bring complaints from people living nearby. Ideally a site for rubbish would be a large area with easy access and where the smell would not matter (either sited well away from housing or next to an accepted existing smell).

There were two established sites which fulfilled these requirement admirably - old gas and sewage works. Normally both industries were sited in out of the way places and were often surrounded by large tracts of waste land. Many old rubbish dumps have been found next to such sites.

Both industries rely on water and would be situated by a river. Sewerage works used the river for the disposal of effluent and gasworks both for the refining process and to help support the gasometers. These waterways solved the twin problems of transportation and access. Before lorries arrived there were only three viable methods for moving large quantities of rubbish - by horse and cart, by boat or by rail. Far more Victorian rubbish was carried by barge (both sail and horse drawn) than any other method. When dump hunting remember that industry has an insatiable appetite for water and abstraction has shrunk previously navigable waterways into small streams, or dried them out completely.

I dug my first bottle from an ex-sewage works site in Surrey. Since then I have dug on similar sites in the Lake District, the Midlands, most of the Home Counties, Sussex, Hampshire and even westwards into Wales. Sewage farms and rubbish dumps seem almost inseparable and I would rate this as the number one place to search for a dump.

Brick works

Millions of bricks used in the construction of Victorian London were produced in the brickfields of Kent, carried up the Medway and Thames by sailing barges which returned loaded with London's rubbish. This was then sifted and the coal ash used in the brick making process.

The finest grade of ash (called soil) was mixed with clay and baked into bricks producing a superior product to clay alone. Coarser ash and small pieces of clinker (breeze) were used as part of the lining of the brick kilns, it was found to distribute the heat more evenly and save on fuel. The remainder of the rubbish (core), including the pots, jars and bottles which we are interested in, was dumped. Some was sold to builders for hard-core, but most was either tipped into the pits from which the brick clay had been excavated, or left in a heap where it had been sifted.

The best known brickworks site in bottle digging was located at Sittingbourne in Kent. It was visited by many thousands of enthusiasts for over 10 years but was put out of bounds when thoughtless diggers started digging the sea wall. Part of the site still remains but anybody caught there will quickly find himself talking to the police.

A large number of brickworks dumps have been discovered in Kent but there are still many more to be found. I have an 1880s list of over 120 companies which produced bricks in this one county alone. Many of these sites are still unexplored today.

Another huge site turned up at Hayes in Middlesex - today it is a vast housing estate complete with marina. The dump was removed for environmental reasons before building work started and the owners gave me permission to search for bottles while this work was in progress. I then worked early mornings and for two years my afternoons were spent picking up items uncovered by the huge diggers removing the dump (It took a further year to catch up on the cleaning).

Bricks were made all over the country and were usually supplied by local manufacturers to save on transport costs. It was also common for construction projects such as railways, bridges, canals and roads to have brickworks built nearby. Many used ash in their bricks and when work ended the clay pits made convenient dumps.

Details of Victorian brick making companies can be found in the old trade gazettes kept in the reference section of main libraries. Modern street maps can be used - look for road names such as Brick Lane or Kiln Road, these may have once carried brickworks traffic. If its location is kept secret a brickworks dump can last a digger for decades.

Canal dumps

Some of Britain's canals are over two hundred years old, the first being built in 1761 by the Duke of Bridgewater to take coal from his mines at Worsley to Manchester. It proved to be a good investment, halving his road transport costs to 6 shillings a ton. During the next 80 years many new canals were built, in some cases freight charges were only a sixth of the cost of carrying it by road.

Canals were made watertight with a thick layer of clay usually being trodden in (or puddled) by driving cattle up and down. To save transport costs the clay for lining and gravel for concrete was often dug out from land lying alongside the intended route. Occasionally brickworks were also built which required even more clay to be dug.

By the mid 1900s a fast and efficient railway network had come into being but freight costs were about twice that of canals. Many railway companies got rid of this competition by buying up canals (or sections of them), then raising the freight charges to an uneconomical level. At this time many of the clay pits dug for the original construction work were still lying open. Faced with losing their livelihoods to the railway companies, many bargees accepted contracts to fill these holes with rubbish from nearby towns.

This method of rubbish disposal was widely used, dumps have been found by the Andover and Bath canals in the South, Swansea to the West, Louth and Horncastle in East Anglia and alongside the Manchester, St. Helens and Rochdale canals in the North. Some London refuse was brought down the river Thames, taken through Brentford lock, then dumped alongside the Grand Union Canal and its various offshoots.

Some redundant canal sections were filled with rubbish and dumps have been discovered in disused waterways in, or near, Halifax, Leeds and Bradford. No doubt there are others still waiting to be found in other parts of the country.

The barges moored next to the dump, unloaded into barrows which were wheeled to tipping areas. Site location is often no more than looking for sections of towpath littered with slivers of broken glass and china which fell during the unloading operation. Old mooring posts might still exist or maybe metal rings set in a concrete lintel alongside the water's edge may give a clue.

If you find telltale signs the next job is to investigate the adjoining land. Check whether the earth or clay surface is natural or could it be capping tipped over the refuse to seal the dump. Look at the ground cover: many canal sites have a good growth of stinging nettles and elderberry trees (both of which thrive on the well-drained acidic soil) with hawthorn trees growing on clay banks.

Some towpaths have been covered with tarmac and made into walks, then it is a matter of looking for changes in the land lying alongside. An obvious case would be where fields adjoining the towpath suddenly run into a large patch of overgrown land. This should be treated as a possible dump.

Around 1970 British bottle digging started on a dump near Iver in Middlesex where the Slough arm joins the Grand Union canal. For the next decade diggers explored the banks of these canals for miles and it was thought that all the local dumps had been discovered. In 1990 a workman told me about large quantities of bottles turning up on a building site next to the canal about 4 miles from Iver. Later that day I arrived at the site just in time to watch an undiscovered Victorian dump being sealed with the last pour of concrete. This dump had remained hidden from diggers for 20 years and, maybe a bit more care in checking would have paid off.

If you have a canal within easy reach then it is worth spending a few days walking its banks, this can make a pleasant outing even if no dumps are found.

Reclaimed land

Those living to the East or Southeast of London have many miles of dump nearby. Large areas of marshland on both sides of the Thames were reclaimed by filling them with Victorian rubbish. The giant Ford Motor Company works at Dagenham is build on Victorian refuse and a huge dump was uncovered in the mid 1980s when work was carried alongside.

The first major reclamation scheme took place around 1875 at Barking Creek, a marshy area adjoining the river Thames. The idea stemmed from Holland where much of the country has been reclaimed from the sea and Dutch engineers were used to oversee the London experiment. The result was so successful that much of the capital's refuse was used to fill Essex marshes and convert them into valuable farmland.

Other city councils copied London's example and land was reclaimed from the Medway in Kent; on parts of Rye harbour; by Southampton water between Marchwood and Totton and the estuaries of the Humber and Orwell in East Anglia. I am certain that many other major rivers around the country have huge sites still awaiting discovery.

Dumps have been found simply by walking along the water's edge at low tide and spotting quantities of broken glass on the foreshore, having been washed out of a waterside dump by past floods - a give-away that there was digging nearby. But finding sites is not always quite so simple as construction work, flood alleviation schemes, new bankings and dredging can make significant changes to the course of a river or its estuary. Reclaimed land may be some distance from today's waterside. I know of one Essex site which now lies half a mile from the river.

This method of disposal is not confined to coastal areas and riversides. Stagnant ponds and inland marshes were also filled with refuse, both to remove an unpleasant eyesore and to destroy the breeding grounds of mosquitoes. Many of those returning from the colonies suffered from malaria, although it was known to be spread by mosquitoes. It was not always realised that the native British insect does not carry the disease.

Reclamation sites can be difficult to identify as the ground is usually level with the surrounding land and there is often no change in the type of undergrowth. Sometimes glass and china will appear in the furrows on farm land when ploughing takes place. But usually, unless there is building work taking place and throwing up bottles, the only way to find a possible site is by research or comparing features on old maps.

Village dumps

Small parish councils could not afford to run rubbish collection services. Either the locals would take their own waste to the dump or a local carter would be used to dispose of refuse - he of course would have made extra money from scavenging. It was not unusual for an out of the way bit of land designated as a dump. This type of site tends to be hidden away (often in woodland), not just for hygienic purposes, sometimes the contractor had to provide his own site and this might have been off the beaten track because he was fly tipping illegally.

Village dumps can be hard to locate but the job can be simplified with a little thought. Rubbish would be carried by horse and cart so there needed to be a track or road to the dump and it is easier to look for this. A copy of an old map is invaluable as any pathways wide enough for a cart will be shown. There may several but some will be for obvious reasons such as routes from a farm to a field used for grazing cattle, or short cuts between the village and a school or church. These should be checked last if a blank is drawn on the others. The track is likely to be overgrown and look like any other woodland, however there may be clues such as a slope from the road or old gateposts may still be standing.

First check routes to quarries and gravel or clay workings, these convenient holes made ideal dumps. If the village lies on a hill check downhill as the carter would have preferred not to transport a heavy load uphill. There may be a stream nearby which would have made a convenient tipping point, or possibly a swamp which was reclaimed.

Location is just a matter of walking the tracks checking for bits of china or glass which fell off the cart as it travelled over the rough ground. If you come across these signs follow them, when they stop the dumping point should be to one side or other of the path. The actual site may have different ground cover or there might still be signs of dumped rubbish as it was normally tipped and left where it lay rather than being buried.

Village dumps tend hold a larger proportion of common items than municipal dumps reflecting the comparable incomes of the inhabitants, but they invariably hold large amounts of local items. Sometimes they are the only source of bottles from a small mineral water supplier or brewery and they can yield previously unrecorded cream pots from a local farm or dairy. They often contain the occasional rarity and if the local squire's rubbish finished up in the dump then it may contain better items than expected.

Village dumps are worth the effort of seeking them out and, as they are likely to be hidden, it should be possible to keep them a secret. But don't sell any items carrying the name of the village until the site is finished. Experienced diggers only need a hint to put them on the trail and you could turn up at your dump to find a gang digging there.

House dumps

Large houses set in their own grounds were unlikely to have received a refuse collection service, waste disposal would have been the responsibility of the householder. Some out of the way area in the grounds may have been set aside as a tip and, although the dump itself may be hard to locate, the likelihood of there being one is self evident as large houses can often be spotted from miles away.

Big houses or stately homes tend to be owned by richer members of society who can afford to buy better quality products and the packaging they discarded should contain more quality items. I would travel a very long way to dig on one of these dumps.

The most common method of disposal was to leave a cart at the back of the house (often near the kitchen), when filled a servant would be detailed to empty it. When seeking out the dump's location try to put yourself in his place. Where would you have dumped a barrow load of rubbish on a winter's day when the weather was being unkind? Bear in mind the following points :-

- It would probably be dumped out of sight from the house.
- It is easier to wheel a loaded cart downhill than up.
- Unless some particular area had been designated as a site the cart was unlikely to be wheeled an inch more than absolutely necessary.
- The bank of a stream makes a good tipping point, it is easier to tip down a slope than on flat ground.
- Sometimes elderberry trees and stinging nettles will have grown on the dump's acidic soil.
- Occasionally rubbish would be buried in the orchard - the vegetable matter provided nutrients, pieces of glass and china helped aerate the soil.
- Flat ground containing marsh plants may indicate that the rubbish has been used to fill in a stagnant pond.
- It may be that the dump is not in the grounds at all but in adjoining woods (check for any signs of an old pathway).

The simplest way of all might be to just ask the owner of the house, or better still - the gardener. A large estate may even have a gamekeeper who will know the grounds like the back of his hand. (Do not forget to show appreciation in the way of a bottle of something).

Building sites

Last century household rubbish was sometimes used as hard-core and many roads, pathways and railway embankments stand on a base of old bottles and jars. This type of site may come to light when work is carried out, such as new buildings or when gas or water pipes are laid.

A basic dump hunting rule is always look down excavated holes and check heaps of earth thrown up by JCBs. It is even possible to spot telltale signs while driving. When M25 widening work was carried out in 1993 it was possible to see a 1930s site on the banking near the M40 junction. On a trip to Scotland I spotted signs of an early dump next to the A74 near Lockerbie where the road was being upgraded. Mechanical diggers had left mounds of earth full of aqua glass and broken china. (I could not investigate due to traffic cones, heavy rain and a rather tired wife.)

It may not be possible to get on a suspected dump when work is taking place, but it might be quiet on weekends. Even if it proves impossible to actually dig, it is worth

Turfs cut and put on polythene sheeting, spoil onto tarpaulins

Nick Magnum (maker of Nikko clay pipes) shows a scarce marmalade pot

Part of the day's haul

Refilling the hole

Turfs replaced and site tidied up

having a word with the digger driver, he is quite likely to pass on any bottles he finds for a reasonable price. If you can get on the site it must be investigated straight away. Next week you could turn up to find the area covered in a layer of concrete. These sites can provide easy digging, often capping having been bulldozed away. I found one which could only be dug on a Sunday when there was no work going on. One week there would be nowhere to dig and the next there was too much to turn over in a day.

Allotments

Our city centres are under pressure from developers and, to preserve an area of open space and parkland "Green Belt" restrictions have been introduced. The situation was rather different during the last century when many city suburbs were still farmland and there was a great deal of land available for building. Since an old rubbish dump could be difficult to develop, it was often left well alone. During the Second World War people were encouraged to grow their own food under the slogan "Dig For Victory". Large tracts of derelict land were cleared or covered in soil and used for this purpose. It is surprising how often allotments are to be found lying on top of old rubbish dumps.

Many allotment sites have now fallen into disuse and they are always worth checking for signs of rubbish. Enamel signs were sometimes used to separate the plots - always check derelict allotment sheds, enamels may have been used in their construction.

"Dug out" sites

Dumps which should never be ignored are the well known ones dug by all and sundry and now thought to be completely finished, these will usually hold untouched areas. Unless a dump is dug in a structured way there are always parts which are missed - the trick is to find them. There are quite a few dumps within easy reach of my home, plus a large number of bottle hunters. Many of the larger sites were extensively dug when the digging hobby first took off, Some reputedly being finished 20 years ago, yet over a third of my digging has been carried out on just these sites.

Probably the best example is the Iver dump in Middlesex which was abandoned by local diggers about seven years before I became involved in the hobby. I have lost count of the number of black and white potlids I have found there (a friend and I dug 102 between us in 10 days) and I have also recovered 8 coloured lids from this site. When I told other club members where I was digging they would not believe me, knowing the site was "dug out" they thought I was making up a story to protect a secret dump elsewhere.

The three main reasons why an area of dump has not been dug are that the digging is unusually difficult, the patch has been covered over or it lies underneath a patch which was only dug to a shallow level. Some areas would be left because nobody fancied fighting their way through a jungle of blackberry bushes or using a pickaxe to go through hard-core. It may have been left because builders rubble had been tipped on top or the capping was unusually thick. I once spent 6 hours digging through 10 feet of clay to reach a very productive seam of Victorian rubbish.

It is surprising how often a heap of spoil by the side of a hole will cover an untouched bit of ground. If this spoil had gone back into the hole at the end of the day then the patch would have been available to dig at a later date.

Often diggers on these large sites did not bother to refill their holes, more commonly they would undercut the sides until it collapsed to leave a shallow crater. When tunnelling out the side of a hole there is a tendency to undercut deeper at the top than the bottom and often, by cutting into the side of an old hole, then digging down, it will reveal virgin dump at quite a shallow level. On going deeper it may turn out that the ground a couple of feet under the original hole is also untouched.

NOTE: Undercutting can be extremely dangerous as it can cause the sides of a hole to collapse on the digger. It must be carried out with a great deal of care (see digging).

Many early diggers did not dig deeply and 4-5 feet seems to be the norm, even on sites **over** 10 feet in depth. This was not through laziness, but at that time there were plenty of dumps around and if digging became too hard on one then they would go elsewhere. Some holes were left because it started raining and everyone went home, or maybe they were dug by kids who could not get to any sort of depth. The only way to find this deeper stuff is to dig a trial hole in the middle of the old one.

This type of site can take a lot of work before anything is found, but I would rather be doing this than sitting at home complaining that there is nowhere left to dig.

Other dumping sites

The previous few pages give some background into the most common methods of rubbish disposal. Reclaimed land, brick works, canal and sewage work sites will generally give the largest areas of digging, but there are plenty of other types of dump, although these tend to be much smaller.

Inns, coaching houses and pubs often had their own dumps, especially in country areas which were often situated near the back door of the building. Village ponds, redundant railway cuttings, backwaters and canals could be refilled and levelled with old rubbish - it may be possible to locate one of these by comparing old maps.

Lime was a commonly used fertiliser and many farmers produced their own by burning chalk. This was normally carried out in kilns sited by the side of the road so that the chalk carts could pull up alongside. When no longer needed these untidy areas made convenient roadside dumps. Furse (gorse) was a favourite fuel and this type of site could possibly be located just by looking for the words "Furse Field" on a map.

There are thousands of disused chalk, rock and slate quarries, all around the country, many provided convenient holes for tipping. Some railway spurs built to take the materials away were also used to bring in the refuse. One dump turned up in Surrey woodland when we checked out a spur shown on a map that was not on a later version.

Owners of clifftop houses often got rid of their refuse by throwing it over the cliff. I have recovered some nice items from the side of a certain Surrey hill which has a large house standing on the top.

If you find some old houses backed by a wall separating them from woodland, a stream or some waste ground, check the area behind the wall. Householders may have solved their rubbish problems by tipping it over the wall.

Rubbish fell into the canals or rivers when barges were being loaded or unloaded and more would have fallen from the carts taking it to a loading point. Thoroughly explore these areas, especially at low tide on a tidal river.

Dumps sometimes turn up when building work is carried out on a school. Although this land was unsuitable for building, if covered with two or three feet of topsoil it could be used as a sports field or play area.

A visit to the reference section of the local library may provide information on other places worth exploring. Local records should show where old potteries, dairies, breweries, glassworks or mineral water works once stood. These firms may have set aside an area for redundant bottles and in some cases, not only is the land now derelict, but old sheds and outbuildings may still stand. Even today these could still contain anything from stocks of bottles or ginger beers to enamel signs, these hoards are still being found. Probably the most remarkable was a find of thousands of Gilbert Rae items (including crates of green top ginger beers) which one lucky hunter found in the derelict factory.

A woman visited the pottery where Clarice Cliff tableware was produced. The area had been levelled but she dug down a few inches and found pieces of broken china with original designs. Although of no use to collectors, imagine the stir it would have caused in the antique world had she found complete items. (She did make a profit by mounting pieces on pins and selling them as badges).

What to look for

Dumps were often covered with a layer of clay or topsoil to reduce the smell and deter insects and rodents. Over the decades trees and bushes grow up and hide any trace of rubbish so that the area now looks very much like any other bit of waste ground. So how can you tell whether or not there is rubbish lying beneath it?

As in all pursuits there is no better way of learning than experience, the more sites that are dug, the more a "feel" for a dump is developed and this sometimes works on a subconscious level. A digging pal was taking his family to Margate for a day at the seaside when he pulled into a lay-by and ran off into some adjoining woods. He had discovered an undug site lying by the side of a busy main road whilst in conversation with his wife. (No he was not allowed to dig, but we went back later and dug it out).

Quoting "experience" is no help at all to a beginner and, whilst it is difficult to put a "feel" into words, it is possible to give pointers as to what to look for. Try to explore possible sites in late winter when the undergrowth has died back so it is possible to see what is under your feet. In the summer undergrowth may be at eye level and grass is likely to be knee high making it impossible to carry out an efficient survey.

Often dumps will have a distinctly different look, there may be humps and hollows whilst surrounding land is flat, or the ground may show a change in colour or texture because capping may have been recovered from a deeper level than the surface soil or brought in from elsewhere. If a suspected dump is at a different level to the surrounding land then any slopes usually have a different look. Natural slopes tend to be well weathered whereas man made slopes are often sharply defined.

Plants and undergrowth found on capping may be different to those growing nearby. The soil is well drained and acidic and stinging nettles and elderberry trees tend to thrive on it. It is a common misconception that all dumps have nettles growing on them, many are grass covered, but patches of elderberries and nettles are always worth checking.

On some dumps the rubbish is still open to view, others may have only been partially capped. It is not unusual for the odd barrow load of rubbish to be fly tipped on

Down to work

Some of the day's results, with
the hole refilled.

top of capping after the site had been abandoned). Even when a site has deep capping some bottles may remain uncovered. Dig some small holes and feel the texture of the earth coming out, natural clay can be moulded when slightly damp, dumped clay has a crumbly or granular texture.

If you suspect you have found a dump but cannot see any trace of rubbish walk round the perimeter, then criss-cross the site using trees and bushes to help work in straight lines. Examine the ground for traces of broken glass and china - you are unlikely to find many complete bottles as frost tends to break them up. Check rabbit holes to see if the animals have burrowed out any traces of ash and look round tree roots for signs of glass or china.

If there are signs that trenches have been dug for pipes or for electricity cables, check these features as well as a couple of yards either side where the spoil would have been heaped prior to refilling. Are there signs that somebody has dug there, maybe years ago? Even if they have refilled their holes they might not have completely hidden all traces of rubbish and could have left the odd bit of aqua glass or broken china lying on the surface.

Ditches or streams running through the site could have rubbish washed into them. Sites have been discovered when pieces of glass and china were spotted lying on the bed of a stream, finding the dump was simply a matter of following the trail of pieces upstream to the point where they had been washed out from the banks. If there is a ditch, see if there are signs of rubbish in any mounds alongside where the contents were left after it was cleaned out.

Obvious signs can save a fair bit of work, otherwise the only way to find out whether there is a dump is to dig trial holes (and go down at least shoulder deep). Even if nothing is found don't immediately give up, you may have hit a deeper bit of capping and a number of trial holes should be taken out in different places.

Probe rod

A considerable amount of work can be saved by using a probe rod (see Tools). Many diggers do not rate them but mine has become a basic part of my digging kit. With a little experience it can be used to tell the depth of capping or whether there is a seam of rubbish beneath it. A few minutes work can locate undug areas on busy sites which are being dug piecemeal.

Even if you do not discover a dump your day may not turn out to be a complete waste of time. If checking the area in the winter, then search the bottoms of any hedges while they are bare. Field workers often tucked empty bottles away in hedgerows to reduce the danger of broken glass to livestock. One lucky Devon collector searching hedgerows in this way discovered a black glass bottle - a complete dated sealed onion 300 years old.

Dating a dump
(Also see chapter on dating bottles)

Having found a site it is important to work out its age, it is pointless digging through stuff that was thrown away thirty years ago, it will not hold many antique bottles. It is not necessary to build up a pile of finds to get an idea of age, an estimate can be made from the first couple of broken botties dug out.

Victorian dumps tend to produce more collectable items than later sites. Machine made bottles started to appear around 1920 and few of these are collected. However, a site from that date is worth digging as things did not change overnight and mould blown bottles will still be found. 1920s dumps yield mineral waters, printed stoneware, ginger beers, medicines, beers, green and blue poisons, plus an occasional potlid. I have had five coloured lids from a local 1925 site.

Even 1930s' tips should not be ignored. Most bottles will be left behind at the end of the day but these sites produce wide mouthed milk bottles, footwarmers, pin cushion dolls and cake decorations, all of which are collectable.

Permission

Once you have found your dump there is one more stage to go through before you can start digging and that is getting permission from the landowner. All land in Britain is owned by somebody and digging without the landowners' permission is illegal and can have severe consequences.

My local council banned bottle digging after local lads had left big holes surrounded by broken glass and china. The first offender caught was fined £25 for breaking a bylaw. A little later a couple more vandals appeared in court, this time the charge was criminal damage and theft and the fine was £200. But this was not the end of it, the council then won a compensation claim against them for restoration of the land. Be warned!!!

Sometimes it will not be possible to trace ownership and that would appear to be the end the matter. If the land is hidden away it may be possible to get away with digging, especially if some flytipping has taken place. But do not complain if you are called to account for your actions. I must confess that, like most long term diggers, I have been on these types of sites in the past. I always refilled the hole and ensured that all broken glass and china was buried. I have even taken "before and after" photos to show that the land was tidier when I had finished. I no longer do this as having to constantly look over your shoulder while digging tends to detract from the fun and my main reason for bottle digging is the enjoyment I get out of it.

It is possible to dig on someone's land by accident. A friend and I paid our first visit to a well-known site and found a flat overgrown area right at the back of the dump where we stared to dig. About half an hour later we were told to clear off by a very indignant lady, it seemed that we were actually digging in her back garden. We went back the next day (with a box of chocolates) and ended up doing a deal. She allowed us to dig for bottles provided we left the ground levelled off so that she could lay a lawn.

The approach

If you owned some land and a complete stranger asked to dig holes in it what would your answer be? A request for permission to dig is more likely to succeed if some thought is given to the initial approach. Always try to make it in person, it is easy to ignore a written request and harder to refuse somebody face to face. If writing then it is good manners to include a stamped self addressed envelope.

Tell the owner that you believe there is a Victorian or Edwardian rubbish dump on his land and that you would like permission to search for old bottles. This is likely to be greeted with incomprehension so point out that, like today, 100 years ago bottles and pots were thrown away when empty. Take along some common bottles as examples (a Codd is excellent as it tends to focus attention). Say that the search may entail digging some small holes and stress that you will only be using a garden fork, not a JCB, and that you will leave the site tidy (photographs of previous digs are useful). If the owner is undecided ask him if you can have a trial dig and come back to him.

Sometimes permission will be granted but conditions laid down, stick to these restrictions. I dug a field in Devon where sheep were gazing and to ensure they came to no harm the turf was laid on polythene and spoil from the dig heaped on tarpaulins. At the end of the day all broken glass was buried when the hole was refilled, the ground tamped down and the turf relayed.

Obtaining permission is harder with company owned land - the problem lies with health and safety laws. If the company grants permission for you to be on their land then they are responsible for your safety and may refuse permission in case you suffer injury and try to claim damages. I always offer a disclaimer stating that I am on the site entirely at my own risk and will not hold them responsible for any loss or injury, no matter how caused. I also have personal injury insurance which also covers me for consequential damage.

Sometimes an enquiry will be met with a flat NO. Just accept that you cannot win them all and file the information away for future reference. Ownerships change and it will do no harm to ask again next year.

Tools of the trade

If you have a garden then you will probably have the basic tools, a fork for loosening up and turning over the earth and a shovel for throwing it out of the hole. Once you become hooked on the hobby it is worth getting some good quality tools. Bottle digging is not the same as turning over a flower bed, it takes a lot of leverage to dislodge a brick from the side of a hole. Don't try to save money by buying the tools on special offer at your local DIY store, few are up to the job. I have had cheap forks fold in half and shovel blades split when bottle digging.

A good fork can make life easier, it should be full size rather than a narrow edging tool, well balance and not too heavy. I recommend the Spear and Jackson Neverbend range, they are a little dearer but have a good weight to strength ratio and have never let me down (although I need to replace them after six months as I tend to wear down the tines with all the digging I do).

Two other necessities are thick soled footwear and a pair of heavy duty gardening gloves. Dump sites are full of razor sharp pieces of broken glass which can cut lightweight shoes to ribbons. Some diggers wear boots but I prefer wellingtons and keep my trouser legs outside to prevent dirt getting in. Hands are working within inches of broken glass embedded in the sides of a hole and heavy duty gloves are vital.

Most serious diggers accumulate a collection of tools which can considerably reduce the amount of effort used in certain situations. Probably the most useful tool is a round ended spade of the type used to bury dead bodies in cowboy films, but fitted with a normal length handle. These take a bit of finding, but are worth having as they cut out 75% of the effort involved when digging gravel and small stones and can often be used in place of a fork. Many Scottish diggers only use this one tool.

A sharp edged spade is invaluable for chopping through roots or slicing into clay and sometimes a pick axe may be required to get through hard-core capping or compacted stones and bricks. On occasions I have even needed to use a sledge hammer on a concrete covered site.

Some dumps are liable to flooding, others have water laying on the clay bed. One of the most frustrating situations is to follow a productive seam of rubbish then find it drops away into water. Digging with standard tools is impossible as items fall between the tines of a fork and wash off a spade or shovel. This problem is overcome with a tarmac fork which has 10 or 12 close set tines.

Lastly, a tool which has proved to be (almost) worth its weight in gold - a probe rod. Many diggers do not use them, but I usually take mine on a dig and it has saved many hours of effort. This tool is a three and a half feet length of quarter inch steel rod with a foot of the same material welded across the top to form a T shape.

Using it is just a matter of pushing it into the ground, and, with just a little experience, it is possible to tell whether there is a seam of rubbish beneath the capping. On well dug site use it on a spoil heap, it will push into the spoil easily and if it then comes up against some resistance then the spoil may be heaped on top of capping. Probe a couple of feet away in several directions and, if it gives the same result, then it is likely that the capping has not been disturbed and is lying on an undug area.

Of course I do not carry all these tools with me every time I go digging. Usually I just take the fork, spade and probe rod, the rest stays in the car boot in case it is needed. When regularly digging a site involving a long walk I often leave the tools hidden in the undergrowth at the end of the day to save carrying them.

Even with careful digging the occasional cuts still occur (my wife says that I would cut myself even if in a suit of armour) so it makes sense to carry some first aid items such as a few plasters, a bit of clean cloth, a pair of tweezers and clean water. (See the "First aid at work" Approved code of practice and guidance from HMSO for further information on first aid materials). Working in dirt means that it is sensible to keep tetanus injections up to date and take some insect repellent spray in summer as mosquitoes and warm weather digging seem to go together.

Before starting

Having located your dump and obtained permission to dig there is a temptation to just race on to the site and start digging. Bottle digging should be fun but it is worth taking a more disciplined approach to ensure that every square inch is dug. If you simply pick a spot and dig, once the hole has been refilled the patch that held the spoil will look just like the area that has been dug and after a few trips you won't know what has been dug and what hasn't.

On new sites it is worth using a probe rod to find the edges of the dump. I like to map out the site using trees, bushes, fences etc to help get a reasonably accurate sketch. One trick is to put a few small twigs in the ground to mark out certain points. If others should find your dump they will probably dive in anywhere and, by marking their holes on your map, it should be possible to find untouched patches once they have abandoned the site believing it dug out.

After refilling the hole at the end of the day mark the corners with twigs. On the next visit dig alongside the previous hole and throw the spoil on top of the dug patch, again mark the dug area at the end of the day. This is a simple means of ensuring that none of the site is missed.

Safety

Over the years several bottle diggers have been buried alive when their holes collapsed on them. A South African digger was killed this way after tunnelling 6 feet into the side of his hole. This sort of action is utter stupidity, no bottle is worth that sort of risk.

Obviously it is not practical to shore the sides of the hole with boards as on building sites and digging must be carried out with some thought to safety. Unless a dump has been capped with loose material such as shingle or sand it is normally quite safe to dig below head height provided that the sides are kept absolutely vertical or sloped in towards the bottom. On loose capped sites an extra couple of feet of material should be removed from around the top of the hole.

Other than the occasional cut, the only danger is the side of the hole collapsing on the digger. On soil covered dumps there is usually some warning which takes the form of a trickle of loose earth which gradually increases in volume until everything falls in. Another sign is a crack in the ground around the hole. If earth starts to trickle into the hole, or a crack appears in the ground above, then get out immediately. It is better to be safe than sorry, no amount of bottles are worth risk to life and limb.

Avoid the temptation to dig into sides when finding the base of a bottle poking out or coming across a thick seam of rubbish. This is dangerous as it weakens the "bearing wall" supporting the weight of the ground above. Never cut into sides if it is intended to dig deeper, these items can be retrieved later.

It is better to dig a decent sized hole as it gives room to get out of the way in the event of a cave-in or something rolling off the spoil heap into the hole. Another safe practice is to have only one tool in the hole at a time. If using the fork, then keep the spade on the top and change them over when you need to shovel out the spoil. If you were to get partly trapped in a collapse then it is possible to reach something to dig yourself out with.

Maybe find a digging partner, in the event of an accident there will be somebody around to help out. Although bottle digging may seem to be as safe as hang gliding, with a little care accidents are unlikely to happen. In 20 years my only accident of note was when I was picking up bottles from a machine dug trench and a clay wall fell on me.

Digging

It would be a shame to find a site then miss areas, this applies as much to depth as the length and breadth and dumps should be dug as deeply as possible. Serious diggers like to scrape the bottom and often go down over 12 feet. Although it is not absolutely vital to get down so deep, with shallow digging the dump under your feet may be lost for ever.

All diggers develop their own technique, I tend to use a fork as much as possible, this being the lightest tool, and only use a shovel when necessary. I prefer to dig a trench some 3 feet wide by 6 feet long - wide enough to prevent elbows from scraping the sides and long enough to step forward for extra leverage to throw out spoil. On grass covered sites the turf can be cut and piled up clear of the hole so it will not get covered by spoil. Capping should then be removed before excavating any of the dump. It is a great temptation to dig down when the first signs of rubbish appear, but will pay to persevere and dig a hole large enough to be worked comfortably.

On sites visited by all and sundry, holes are often dug and left. Starting is easier if you get into one of these old holes and cut into the side, less effort is needed to throw spoil behind than to lift it before throwing it out.

Some dumps have very hard capping, the easiest way to get through this is to dig a small hole until below this hard layer, undercut until it falls down, then shovel out. Clay capping can be a problem to get through, it is either so hard that it almost needs a pickaxe, or so soft that is has to be scraped off a shovel. Again the undercut and shovel method is the easiest way to open up a hole.

A common question is "Do you break a lot digging?". Old bottles are surprisingly tough and it is surprising how little does get broken, unfortunately Sod's Law ensures that quality items break easier than common ones. One precaution against damage is not to lever out bottles, the fork's tines might break it or scratch the surface. Instead gently loosen up the ground packed around it and lift it out by hand.

When starting, throw the spoil as far back as possible, as it piles up it slides and spreads out. If the spoil heap is close to the hole it will constantly fall back in and it wastes energy to shovel it further back. Occasionally check the spoil heap, no matter how carefully digging is carried out items can be thrown out with the waste material. I dig faster when my wife accompanies me as it then is just a matter of continuous shovelling, I pick up finds from the hole and she checks what is thrown out.

Once the capping has been removed there are often quite a lot of items found in the top foot or two, finds then tend to be somewhat sparser until just above the bottom of the dump. Rubbish settles over the years and often the thickest seam of rubbish is found just above the bed. Heavy items tend to sink into this layer and the seam of compacted stoneware and bottles can be two feet thick.

If you come across a layer of sand or clay try digging through it, this could be a false bed covering another layer of dump. It was common practice to cover various layers as tipping took place. I have one local site some which, in places, has six layers of capping. The bottom of a dump is usually distinctive, often consisting of solid clay, gravel, or maybe a layer of stones or builders rubble, on reclaimed marshland dump it often consists of a smelly goo.

Once you reach the bed turn over the bottom foot of this, if rubbish was tipped in wet weather items may have sunk into the bed. Before finishing use the probe a rod to see if it is the actual base or just another layer of capping with another (maybe older) dump underneath.

When digging a virgin dump the ash has distinct changes of colour where the various layers of rubbish have been tipped, these are most commonly shades of grey, yellow or red. Roots from surface plants can go down a considerable distance. On sites which has been dug for some time novices can spend a lot of time turning over previously dug patches, this situation should not occur with a little experience. If you are not finding bottles and digging a uniformly coloured ash, especially if a fairly loose texture, then it is likely that the patch has already been dug. The act of turning over the ground will have mixed the colours together, usually to a uniform grey. Another clue to previous digging is that it will have thin tendrils running through it rather than proper roots.

Once the hole has been dug, the bottom turned over and finds packed away, it is time to fill it in again. This refilling can be rather a chore at times but restoration should be carried out as a matter of course. The land which has provided enjoyment should be treated with respect. Before shovelling any spoil back into the hole recover bottles poking out of the sides. But do not just pull them out anyhow, there is still a danger of the side collapsing. It is still possible to do some more digging and collect these items in safely by undercutting. This must be carried out carefully, undercutting too deeply can be extremely dangerous, the walls bear the weight of the ground above and great care must be taken. Anybody at the bottom of a ten feet hole stands a good chance of being buried if this happens, but it is possible to undercut for a foot or so quite safely.

My method is to tunnel out the ends of the hole (note **ends**, not **sides**). Starting at the bed of the dump spread spoil along the trench so that it gradually fills from the bottom. As it becomes shallower this is the time to pull out items from the sides of the hole. It is normally possible to use the undercut and spread method until just below the capping before there is a danger of the top falling in.

NEVER undercut on a site with clay capping. There is rarely any warning that a collapse is imminent and clay is very heavy, a big lump falling 6 ft is likely to damage anybody it lands on.

Ideally when digging, capping is put on one side of the hole, and spoil on the other and broken bottles and large pieces of china at the ends. On refilling, the bigger bits are the first to go back to make sure that they are well and truly buried, next comes the spoil, followed by the capping and finally the turf replaced. If the owner turns up and sees his property looking like a World War 1 battlefield he will probably slap an immediate ban on bottle digging. This has happened all too often and many good dumps which have been lost due to thoughtlessness (or laziness) by a small minority of diggers. In some cases the hobby has suffered adverse publicity in local papers giving the public an impression that bottle diggers are vandals.

Although refilling should be seen as the norm, there are some sites where it is not necessary to level the ground after digging. These dumps are usually larger ones visited by diggers from far and wide who, instead of refilling their holes, simply undercut all round until the sides collapse to leave a shallow crater. (The spoil heap is usually left where it was thrown and often covers virgin dump which can be dug at a later date, once these visitors have left thinking the site to be "dug out".)

As with most hobbies it is easy to get hooked and carried away which may not go down too well with the rest of the family. Why not treat it as a day out and take a picnic - they may even get interested themselves.

Cleaning on site
(See also appendix 1)

The job can be made easier if the cleaning process is started on site. Usually dirt adhering to a bottle is slightly damp when it comes out of the ground. Most of this can be removed by wiping with a bit of rag before it has a chance to dry out. Dirt inside the bottle can be shaken out and the big lumps often found inside wide mouth jars can usually be broken up with a stick. I have got into the habit of carrying out this initial cleaning when I take a break for a drink or a bite to eat. Another advantage of wiping down finds on the site is that they can be inspected for damage, these rejects can be immediately discarded, much better than carrying home useless items.

Another tip is to take the stoppers out of internally threaded beers and mineral waters. Sometimes they give off a strong "yeasty" aroma and it is better to get rid of any pungent smell on the dump rather than indoors.

The best of the day's finds

Appendix 1: Cleaning Bottles

I like to have bottles in as good a condition as possible and I am often asked why they look so clean. (I once overheard a tourist tell his friend that they could be made to look old if they were rubbed with sandpaper). There is no magic formula that can make bottles in poor condition look like new. However, with a little knowledge and bit of work most items can be cleaned provided they are in good condition to start with.

Over the years I have developed a cleaning system that works for the large quantities of bottles that I accumulate and the following information is based on my own methods. It is **likely** that equally good results can be had with some of the vast range of proprietary cleaners on the market, so it is worth experimenting.

N.B. - NEVER mix cleaners as the chemical reaction could give out dangerous or toxic fumes. Test out a product on a reject bottle and if it works then of course use it.

Sickness

When a bottle is buried for many years the glass can be abraded by acids in the soil which remove a few molecules from its surface. This usually appears as an area of dullness or a milky wash over part or all of the bottle which magically disappears when wet but comes back as soon as the bottle dries out. It is impossible to remove at home, no matter what household chemicals are used or how much it is worked on. This very common condition is known as "sickness" and collectors tend to look on the majority of sick bottles as having little or no value.

Most beginners are unaware of this and buy items in good faith only to be disappointed when they wash them. I believe that it is unethical for dealers not to explain the condition when selling sick bottles to obvious newcomers to the hobby.

Occasionally I have been asked if I wish to buy collections which have cost the owner a fair amount of money and have felt embarrassed in rejecting them due to their poor condition. Sick bottles can only be improved by polishing or treating with special acids. This is a skilled job using dangerous chemicals which are not available to the general public and must only be used under controlled conditions. The process can be expensive and while it may be worth paying out to have a rarity treated, it is cheaper to replace a common bottle with a better example.

In extreme cases enough of the surface is removed to give the glass a rainbow effect known as opalescence. Whilst sick bottles often have little or no value, multi-coloured examples of even common bottles can be more collectable the those in perfect condition.

If you have a sick bottle that you are particularly fond of then its condition can be disguised by wiping it over with a little oil or by giving it a thin coat of varnish (either by painting or spraying). The bottle will look a lot better on a shelf but is easily recognised as being treated when handled. Never try to sell a doctored bottle as it can result in the loss of any reputation for honest dealing.

Equipment

Do not carry out cleaning in the kitchen sink. No matter how well you clean up after you have finished the dirt will discolour a work surface and the grit will leave scratches. It is far better to use plastic buckets or even an old baby bath for cleaning. Always bear in mind that although you may be cleaning a mineral water bottle you have no idea what might have been put in the bottle at some stage in its life. It may have been used to hold some poisonous or caustic substance so for safety's sake always wear rubber gloves.

The tools needed are cheap and fairly easy to find. Most important is a selection of bottle brushes. Some types have half an inch of wire at the end which makes it difficult to get into corners so try to find ones with bristles coming right down to the end of the brush. The tiny brushes used for cleaning the spouts of tea pots are ideal for small bottles such as perfumes and inks. I usually buy brushes from hardware shops rather than chemists as they generally have a larger selection and tend to be cheaper. I have even found a couple of radiator brushes that reach the bottoms of even the longest bottles.

Coloured nylon scouring pads, about 6 by 4 inches, are perfect for scrubbing the outsides of bottles and jars. DO NOT USE Wire wool or Brillo pads as they scratch glass or salt glazed stoneware and can do irreparable damage the surface of glazed items.

A couple of other useful tools are a letter opener with a long thin blade which can be used to cut up corks which have been pushed inside bottles and an old toothbrush which is especially useful for cleaning the grooves on poisons.

The condition of bottles dug from a Victorian rubbish tip

Cracks and chips

Small chips and nicks are fairly common on dug bottles, they may have been thrown into a bin, from there to a cart, into a barge, back on another cart, then tipped into a hole in the ground. It is rather surprising that glass could stand this treatment without being broken into small pieces, but many do survive intact and the occasional small blemish is only to be expected. When buying it is up to the purchaser to decide whether this sort of minor damage is acceptable.

Cracks are entirely different - something to steer clear of however small they are. Changes in temperature, the vibrations from passing traffic and the change in cabin pressure if the bottle flies home with a foreign tourist will all work to enlarge the crack and the likely outcome is that the bottle will fall to pieces.

Washing

Freshly dug bottles have been buried for many years under constant pressure from the ground surrounding them. If they are taken straight home and put into warm water there is a risk of breakage due to the stresses set up by the sudden change in temperature. To reduce this risk they should be given a day or two to acclimatise before treatment.

If a bottle is still sealed with a cork or stopper then open it outside. It can take hours to get rid of the smell from a bottle in which the dregs have fermented for 100 years.

The first stage is to immerse the bottles in luke-warm water and leave them for a while to soften up any dirt adhering to them. If cleaning glass bottles or salt glazed stoneware it is worth adding a generous measure of bleach which aids the process (do not use bleach on glazed items). Some diggers soak their finds for 24 hours in a solution of water and household soda crystals (**not** caustic soda).

After a good soak, transfer your bottles to a bucket of clean water and give them a thorough scrub to remove as much dirt as possible. Some items will require no more treatment other than a final rinse in **clean** water. Others will have rust, iron or some other stubborn stains which will not move just by washing, but don't despair, it is possible to get rid of most stains, although it may take some time.

Cleaning methods vary amongst diggers, some fill them with various solutions such as weak acids or bleaches, I have one friend who swears by lavatory cleanser to remove certain stains. Another has a penchant for boiling his finds on the kitchen stove, but both this and the use of dishwashers, are rather too drastic for my tastes.

One tip is to put a handful of gravel and some water in the bottle and shake vigorously as a way of cleaning the inside, but this could cause damage if there is an air bubble lying just under the surface. Some people clean the outside of a bottle by pushing it into a bucket of soft sand and rotating it, although this should not be done too vigorously as it may scratch the surface.

Further cleaning

There are some stains which can be dealt with fairly easily. The tar like deposit inside bottles such as cough cures can be removed by filling it with paint stripper and leaving for five minutes (the stripper can be re-used several times) then cleaning with brushes and lots of changes of water. Rust can often be removed using the proprietary rust removers found in any car spares shop.

Occasionally a white glazed item will be found with a dull grey finish which has probably been caused by smoke. This can be treated with Hydrogen Peroxide which is obtained from any chemist. Put the item in an airtight box (one or two litre ice cream containers are ideal) cover with peroxide and leave it to work. Sometimes the item will come white after a couple of hours, at other times it can take two weeks. Once cleaned, soak in frequently changed water to get all traces of peroxide out of the glaze.

Bleach

Bleach has always been a recognised cleaning agent amongst bottle diggers but its effectiveness appears to have been reduced a few years ago when its formula was changed to make it more biodegradable. Thick bleaches may kill all known germs but, even when diluted, it does not penetrate the minute cracks in a glazed surface which hold the dirt. It tends to cling to the surface of a pot, achieving very little. For bottle cleaning I use cheap economy bleach which seems to be more effective and saves on cost.

With glass bottles some stains will loosen up if left in a bucket of water to which a bottle of bleach has been added. I use a small plastic rubbish bin with an airtight lid for the large quantities that I clean. Neat bleach can be used on especially stubborn marks in glass and bottles can be safely left to soak for a couple of days (or even weeks). The bleach will slowly act on the stain without affecting the glass in any way.

One idea for reducing the amount needed to treat the occasional bottle is to stand it in a plastic lemonade or cola bottle which has had the top cut off, just pour in sufficient bleach to fill and cover the item. The container can be covered with a polythene bag secured with an elastic band to reduce the smell.

After several weeks of use bleach has a tendency to separate, but even this can be utilised, I just pour it into a bin in which items with especially stubborn stains can sit for a couple of months. Glass bottles will only need washing a couple of times in clean water to get rid of the bleach, but special care is needed for other materials.

With stoneware start with a weak bleach solution, it is much better to gently remove a stain over a long period rather than to attempt to force it quickly with harsh treatment. Give the item a daily scrub in warm water and return it to the solution. I am not sure that it does any good but a daily inspection means that it does not soak any longer than is absolutely necessary.

Note - Bleach will rot stoneware and china if it is not completely removed from the glaze and your treasures could crumble away into dust in a few months. **All traces** of bleach must be removed from stoneware, do not try to short cut this stage.

My method is to give the items a scrub in warm water, change the water and give them a second wash to remove the surface bleach. The next stage is to put them in a bucket of hot water, after a couple of hours change the water and repeat this process. Do this three or four times a day until there is no smell of bleach on the item. Although I use ordinary tap water, others recommend the use of distilled water. A good general rule is to soak items for a longer period than they have been in treatment. Although I have not tried it, I am told that bleach can be neutralised by using salt in the water.

Acid

There is one final stage which can be tried if all else fails which is to use a weak (30%) solution of hydrochloric acid. This is sold by some hardware shops under the name

Spirits of Salts and it should be diluted even further by adding it to an equal amount of cold water. Always **add acid to water** rather than water into acid, this way if any drops splash up from the container they will be predominantly water.

Spirits of salts can only be sold by outlets licensed by their local authority, some of which charge shopkeepers a lot of money and place restrictions on storage. Consequentially it may not be sold in some areas and, if you can find it then may prove rather expensive. A good alternative can be obtained from some builders merchants in the form of a weaker solution called brick acid, used for cleaning grime out of brickwork. I have also seen paving and patio cleaner in some of the large DIY superstores. This is only a 15% acid solution and should be ideal for cleaning bottles.

Warning - hydrochloric acid can be dangerous. It is an excellent cleaning agent but the pungent fumes could can damage the lungs and it will cause irritation if splashed on exposed skin. Always wear rubber gloves and eye protectors, store in airtight plastic containers and keep it out of out house away from children and pets. It might be better to live with a stain rather than risk using this.

Light stains may only need a couple of hours soaking but heavier staining may require a few days. After treatment (as with bleach) it is absolutely imperative that all traces of acid are flushed out with frequently changed clean water. Glass bottles will only need to be rinsed a couple of times and saltglaze should be OK after a couple of changes of water. Glazed items need to soaked **at least** as long as they have been in the acid. As with bleach, if it is not completely flushed out then the glaze may lift and destroy the item.

Especially stubborn stains may require a number of treatments, soak in bleach and flush out, then in acid, again followed by soaking in water, then back to bleach. I have had items which have taken the best part of a year to come clean.

After cleaning I usually put treated items pots into a "quarantine" box in my airing cupboard for a couple of weeks and they are regularly inspected to make sure that all traces of chemical have been removed. If acid remains in the glaze it will have a yellowish tinge and bleach leaves a powdery deposit. Any signs of either means that the item goes through the flushing process again.

Finishing off

The final stage of any cleaning is to wash inside and out in clean lukewarm water. If the final rinse is carried out in dirty water then it leaves a fine film of dirt on the item when the water dries out.

If the item is destined for your collection why not give it a shine before putting it on the shelf? Stoneware comes up well with a quick squirt of furniture polish, then buffing up with a duster. Glassware can be polished with most proprietary furniture polishes, but for a really outstanding finish try using shoe polish of a matching colour (use neutral on aqua glass), again buffed up with a duster.

A word of warning - take care with handling as they can be rather slippery when polished.

Appendix 2: Dating Bottles

The accurate dating of bottles can be very difficult and in many cases impossible, few items carry a date and the same bottle may have been used by a firm for decades. Any date shown may not necessarily be that of manufacture, but could be when the company was established or even when that particular type of bottle was first made. The best that can normally be hoped for is a period during which a particular item was used.

The well-known marmalade pot of James Keiller is a good example of both the ease and the difficulty of accurate dating. Early examples are found which carry a date 1862 and these were used until 1873 when the company won a gold medal at the Vienna Exhibition. The date 1873 was then added to the design and the shape of the pot and trademark design remained much the same until around 1930.

The shape of a bottle, the crudeness of manufacture, thickness of glass, pontil mark, style of embossing, shape of lip or string rim, colouration and type of mould used can all help give some clues as to when an item was probably produced. The only way to learn about this is to look at, ask about and best of all, handle as many bottles as possible. Having dug tens of thousands of items straight out of the ground from accurately dated dumps, I am usually willing to make a guess at the period in which a bottle was produced. But even with this background any estimate will only be a probability based on personal experience and could be wrong.

Any numbers marked on stoneware are usually just pattern or batch numbers even if they look like dates. This may seem rather negative but there are times when it is possible to give an item an actual date of manufacture. The two figure number found in the pottery stamp of many Bourne of Denby pieces is actually the last two digits of the date. (e.g. 98 is 1898 and 21 would be 1921). Since Joseph Bourne was once the largest supplier of stoneware in the country, it is likely that an old rubbish tip will contain some of his products and means that an indication of the dump's age can be gained from even the smallest fragment bearing a pottery mark.

Sometimes today's collectables appear in the photos or advertising in old magazines, newspapers, catalogues and trades journals and these can be an invaluable source of reference. Not only do they show when an item was used, but will identify the contents, although it should be borne in mind that suppliers may have used standard shaped bottles for a wide variety of products.

Research can reveal when a firm closed down or changed its trading name or address and this information will help identify the earliest or latest date for an item. For example, John Gosnell who used a profile of the young Victoria on their cherry toothpaste potlids well into the 1920s, became a limited company in 1903 and therefore any showing the name John Gosnell and Co. Ltd. must be after that date.

Today's problems with pirating designs are nothing new. It has long been common practice to cash in on popular products and 150 years ago competitors often gave their products similar tradenames and copied packaging (Bovril once had Bovil as a competitor). From 1842 companies could get three years' protection on designs by registering them with the Patent Office. Registration details would be shown on the item and, although this will not give the actual date of manufacture, it does indicate the earliest possible date an item was made and a likely period of use.

Between 1842 and 1883 the registration mark was in the form of a diamond

(Registration Diamond) and is found on both stoneware and glass bottles. Unfortunately, due to the crude manufacturing methods and amount of detail involved, they can sometimes be difficult to decipher. Originally the letter in the top corner denoted the year of registration, but when all the letters of the alphabet had been used it became necessary to move this to the right hand side.

Patent Office Registration Marks

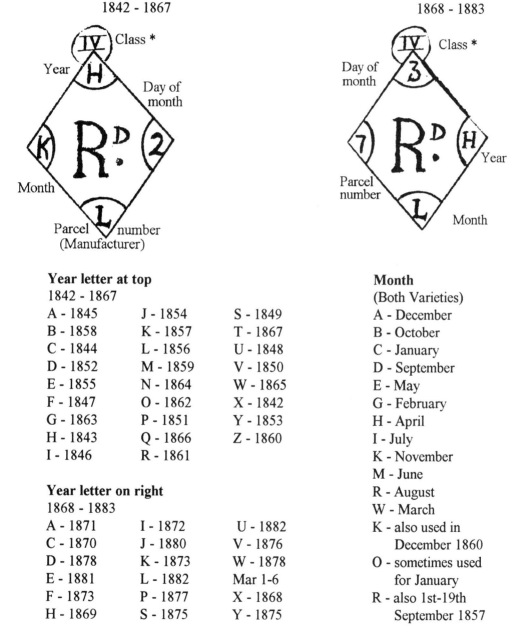

1842 - 1867

1868 - 1883

Year letter at top
1842 - 1867

A - 1845	J - 1854	S - 1849
B - 1858	K - 1857	T - 1867
C - 1844	L - 1856	U - 1848
D - 1852	M - 1859	V - 1850
E - 1855	N - 1864	W - 1865
F - 1847	O - 1862	X - 1842
G - 1863	P - 1851	Y - 1853
H - 1843	Q - 1866	Z - 1860
I - 1846	R - 1861	

Year letter on right
1868 - 1883

A - 1871	I - 1872	U - 1882
C - 1870	J - 1880	V - 1876
D - 1878	K - 1873	W - 1878
E - 1881	L - 1882	Mar 1-6
F - 1873	P - 1877	X - 1868
H - 1869	S - 1875	Y - 1875

Month
(Both Varieties)
A - December
B - October
C - January
D - September
E - May
G - February
H - April
I - July
K - November
M - June
R - August
W - March
K - also used in
    December 1860
O - sometimes used
    for January
R - also 1st-19th
    September 1857

* Class - There were 13 classes, or types, of goods, those covering bottles are III for glass and IV for ceramics.

Once all the available letters had been used a second time the Patent Office changed their recording system to a simple register. No.1 being issued on 1 January 1884 for the Triangle trademark of Bass Brewery.

The registration number can be shown with a variety of prefixes:-
Registration Number; Reg No; R.D; Reg; Reg Design; RAN; etc. The list shown below gives the number be issued on the 1 January each year.

Patent Office Registration Numbers

1	1884	185713	1892	351202	1900	518415	1908
19754	1885	205240	1893	368154	1901	534963	1909
40480	1886	224720	1894	385088	1902	552000	1910
64520	1887	246975	1895	402913	1903	673750	1920
90483	1888	246975	1896	425017	1904	751160	1930
116648	1889	291241	1897	447548	1905	837520	1940
141273	1890	311658	1898	471486	1906	860854	1950
163767	1891	331707	1899	492487	1907		

Further information on registered designs and patents can be obtained from: The Public Records Office, Ruskin Avenue, Richmond, Surrey, TW9 4DU.

Other than early glass and coloured potlids, bottle collecting is usually seen as being a world apart from "proper" antiques. However the following clues for establishing the earliest possible date for an antique apply equally as well to bottles. The word Limited (or Ltd, Ld) was not used until after 1860 and then only rarely before 1880. Trade Mark was used after the Trades Mark Act of 1862. The use of Royal or a picture of the Royal Coat of Arms indicates Victorian or later. The word England was used from 1875, but is more common after 1891 when the American McKinley Tariff Act was passed, this decreed that imports must be marked with their country of origin. The markings Bone China, English Bone China or Made in England all indicate 20th century.

For those like myself with a mental block on dates (I once bought a present for my wife and was rather surprised when she told me it was actually my birthday, not hers), shown below are the dates for the collecting periods used in antiques.

Tudor
Henry VII   1485 - 1509
Henry VIII   1509 - 1547
Edward VI   1547 - 1553
Mary   1553 - 1558
Elizabethan
Elizabeth I   1588 - 1603
Stuart or Jacobean
James I   1603 - 1625
Charles I   1625 - 1649
Commonwealth
Cromwell   1649 - 1660
Carolean or Restoration
Charles II   1660 - 1685
James II   1685 - 1689

William & Mary Regency
William & Mary 1689 - 1702
Queen Anne
Anne   1702 - 1714
Georgian
George I   1714 - 1727
George II   1727 - 1760
George III 1760 - 1820
Regency
Although George was only Regent from 1811-1820, this period is normally taken as being 1800 - 1830.
George IV 1820 - 1830

William IV 1830-1837
Victorian and later
Victoria   1837 - 1901
Edward VII 1901 - 1910
George V   1910 - 1936
Edward VIII 1936
(Abdicated after 325 days)
George VI   1936 - 1952
Elizabeth II 1952 to present

Appendix 3: Bottle Clubs

Some thirty years ago, in the early days of bottle collecting a national bottle collectors club was set up. This was due to the efforts and enthusiasm of the most famous bottle digger of all time Edward Fletcher. Within a few years the club had become far too big for one man to oversee and he split the organisation into regional clubs under the management of local enthusiasts.

Since then many of the regional clubs have died off due to lack of interest whilst others have gone from strength to strength and now form the backbone of the hobby. It is not unusual for a club to appear on the scene to cater for local interest when a large digging site is found and inundated by dozens of bottle diggers. Once the site is finished most of these clubs die out, only to reappear when another dump is found.

As I write this there are around three dozen bottle clubs dotted around the country. The details shown below are those for established clubs or those that are likely to be around for the foreseeable future. For membership information or details of meetings a contact name is shown (if writing, an S.A.E. would be appreciated).

ALTON BC: Mick Wells, 16 Moreland Close, Alton, Hants GU23 2SA.

AMBER VALLEY BC: Richard Evison. 21 Lake Avenue, Loscoe, Derbyshire.

AVON BC: Sue Arthur. Tel: 0117-955-6644 (evenings)

BRIGG B&CC: Brian Ashwell: 33, Yarrow Road, Grimsby, N.E.Lincs, DN34 4JT. Tel: 01472-350653

BUCKS B & BC: John Brown, 4 Dumas Close, Bicester, Oxon OX6 8FT.

BURY BC: Harry Wylie. Tel: 0161-797-4442 (up to 9.30 pm)

CHESTERFIELD OB & CC: Paul Vann. Tel: 01246-239425

COLCHESTER B & CC: Martin Bloomfield, 47 Winstree Road. Stanway, Colchester, Essex.

CORNWALL BCC: Henry Grattan, Grattan Grange, Wenford Bridge, Bodmin PL30 3PN. Tel: 01872-73763

CUMBRIA ABC Martin Nicholl, Swan Cottage, Ireby, Carlisle. Tel: 016973-71208.

DORSET AB & CC: Andrew Lane,32, Main Street, Broadmayne, Dorchester DT2 8EB. Tel: 01305-854965.

EAST ANGLIA BC: Peter Holmes, Talsarn, Market St, Tunstead, Norwich NR12 8RB.

EXETER ABC: Sue Hunt, Flat 4, The Old Bell House, Market Square, Axminster, Dorset.

GLOUCESTERSHIRE BCC: Bruce Wright, 17 Okus Rd, Charlton Kings, Cheltenham, Gloucs.

INVICTA (KENT) BCC: I. Scadden, 25 Russett Way, Swanley, Kent. Tel: 01322-660751

LEICESTER ACC: J. Feast, 5 Fox Hollies, Sharnford, Nr. Hinckley, Leics. LE10 3PH.

MORAY ABCC: Ian Gosling, 21 Mill Road, Nairn. Scotland IV12 5EP.

NORTHERN IRELAND ABC: David Scott, 52 Ormiston Cresc, Belfast B74 3JQ.

NORTHUMBERLAND & DURHAM BCC: D. Robertson, 61 Blanchland Ave, Wideopen, Newcastle upon Tyne.

OXFORDSHIRE BCC: Dorothy Ives Tel: 0993-898388

PLYMOUTH OBC: Roger Wood Tel: 01752-773417 or 01752-34472

SOUTH WALES ABC: Jeff Dunscombe, 76 Hill View, Cardiff, S. Wales.

SOUTH YORKSHIRE ABC: 2 Strafford Ave, Elsecar, Barnsley, S.Yorks, S74 8AA.

STOCKPORT B MEET: Tel: 0161-486-0927

SURREY BCC: K. Wicks, 2 Dairy Cottages, Denbies Estate, Ranmore Common, Dorking, Surrey, RH5 6SP.

TRENT VALLEY BC: Diana Snowden. Tel: 01623-824167. Caters for collectors in the midlands.

WARWICKSHIRE BC: Phil Robbins, 5 Normandy Close, Hampton Magna, Warwick.

WITHAN BC: Dave Marshall. Tel: 01636-676585.

Thanks to the *British Bottle Review* for assistance in compiling the above list.

Appendix 4: Museums

Some of these museums have bigger collections of bottles than others. We would recommend phoning first if looking for particular items or collections.

Alby Bottle Museum, Alby Craft Centre, Cromer Road, Erpingham, Norwich, NR11 7QE. Tel: 01263-761327.

The Bass Museum, Horningen Street, Burton upon Trent, Staffs, DE14 1TQ. Tel: 01283-511000.

Bath Industrial Heritage Centre, Camden Works, Julian Road, Bath, BA1 2RH. Tel: 01225-318348.

Birmingham Museum of Science and Industry, Newhall Street, Birmingham B3 1RZ. Tel: 0121-235-1661.

Bottle Museum, Codswallop Trust, Elscar Heritage Centre, Nr Barnsley, S Yorkshire, S74 8HT Tel: 01226 745156. Fax: 01226-361561

Buckleys Yesterdays World, 90, High Street, Battle, East Sussex, TN33 0AQ. Tel: 01424-775378 (information) or 01424-774269

Flambards Village, Helston, Cornwall, TR13 0QA. Tel: 01326-564093 (24 hour).

"How We lived then", Museum of Shops & Social History, 20, Cornfield Terrace, Eastbourne, E. Sussex, BN21 4NS. Tel: 01323-737143.

National Bottle Museum, Elsecar Heritage Centre, Near Barnsley, S.Yorkshire. Tel: 01226-745156. Fax: 01226-361561.

National Glass Centre, Liberty Way, Sunderland, SR6 0GL. Tel: 0191-515-5555.

Robert Opie Collection, Museum of Advertising & Packaging, Albert Warehouse, Gloucester Docks, Gloucester, GL1 2EN. Tel: 01452-302309.

Flambards Village, Helston, Cornwall
Bottle collectors paradise

- Hundreds of interesting Bottles on display in original settings
- Flambards' Internationally Acclaimed Victorian Village, over 50 shops, homes and traders
- First and Original Life Size Britain in the Blitz street complete with homes and shops
- Chemist Shop Time Capsule - seen just as it was locked away and forgotten nearly 90 years ago

FLAMBARDS VILLAGE, HELSTON, CORNWALL TR13 OQA
24 Hr Infoline 01326 564093

Discover more about bottles and related items by joining the UK's best bottle club

The Surrey Bottle Collectors' Club

run by collectors for collectors

The club has been established for over 20 years and has a reputation as one of the most innovative, active and well run of its kind in the UK.

The club meets on the last Saturday of the month (excluding December) at the Parish Church Hall, Church Road, Leatherhead, from 7pm; and holds an annual bottle and collectors' fair in the autumn.

Here are some of the many advantages of being a member.

- Free trade tables at meetings/ buy-sell-swap
- Free use of extensive library
- Free public liability insurance for diggers
- Monthly competitions
- Display competitions
- Interesting talks from guest speakers
- New finds evenings - friendly, witty and informative
- Annual bottle show, with concessionary table rates for members
- Free quarterly colour newsletter
- Entitlement to shares in the club including 'credits' which can reduce future subscriptions
- Christmas party
- Annual club outing to places of interest

Membership annual subscriptions (1998/99)
Family membership £10.50
Adult membership £7.00
Junior membership (under 16) £3.50

If you would like to join, please write giving your name and address and telephone number etc, enclosing your remittance payable to:
The Surrey Bottle Collectors' Club.
Send to: Mrs Ann Wheeldon, Membership Secretary, Surrey Bottle Collectors' Club, 146 Banstead Road, Caterham, Surrey CR3 5QF.
For further details about the club contact the Club Secretary Mrs Kae Wicks, 2 Dairy Cottages, Denbies Estate, Ranmore Common, near Dorking, Surrey RH5 6SP.

Sports Books from London League Publications Ltd

The Sin Bin

A new collection of Rugby League cartoons and
humour. Caricatures of leading people in the game
... the Adventures of Mo ... The Flatcappers... Bath v Wigan
... Life Down South ... and much more. **Price: £5.95.**
Special offer: £5.00. Published in October 1996.

Touch and Go
A History of Professional Rugby League in London

From the clubs in the 1930s to the London Broncos. Includes all the
international matches played in London, and the first Wembley Cup Final.
. Many photos and illustrations, and comprehensive statistics.
Published August 1995. 380 pages for just £9.00.
SPECIAL OFFER: £5.00 ONLY.

From Arundel to Zimbabwe
**A Cricket Followers' Guide to British and
International Cricket Grounds**

Tries in the Valleys
**A history of Rugby League
in Wales**

Detailed information about
all British First class grounds,
and international test grounds.
Over 30 photos, local maps and
descriptions of grounds.
Cost: £6.50. Now just £5.00
Published in April 1997.

Published April 1998.
£14.95 post free.

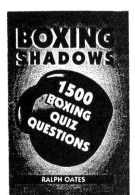

Boxing Shadows:
1,500 Boxing Quiz Questions
Test your boxing knowledge! Questions for all levels of
knowledge. Written by boxing quiz specialist Ralph Oates.
Published in September 1997 at £6.95. **SPECIAL OFFER:**
£6.00 post free.

To order any of the above books, make cheques payable to:
London League Publications Ltd, and send to: London League
Publications Ltd, PO Box 10441, London E14 0SB. All books
post free.